PERELANDRA MICROBIAL BALANCING PROGRAM MANUAL

PERELANDRA MICROBIAL BALANCING PROGRAM MANUAL

Machaelle Small Wright

PERELANDRA

CENTER FOR NATURE RESEARCH
JEFFERSONTON ✿ VIRGINIA

FIRST PRINTING

Copyright © 1996 by Machaelle Small Wright

For information, write Perelandra, Ltd.

This book is manufactured in the United States of America.

Designed by Machaelle Wright and James F. Brisson.

Cover design by James F. Brisson, Williamsville, VT 05362.

Copy-editing by Elizabeth McHale, Stamford, VT 05352.

Production assistance by Clarence N. Wright.

Formatting, typesetting and computer wizardry
by Machaelle Wright.

A special thank you to the 1996 Perelandra staff for helping me iron out the kinks in
the Microbial Balancing Program and this manual. They have saved readers a number of headaches.
I also thank Dr. Albert Schatz for providing technical information about microbes
and their impact on the human body.

This book was formatted, laid out and produced
using the Corel Ventura Publisher software along with
the Hewlett Packard Laser Jet 4 printer.

Printed on recycled paper.

Published by Perelandra, Ltd.,
P.O. Box 3603, Warrenton, VA 20188

Library of Congress Card Catalog Number: 95–092802
Wright, Machaelle Small
Perelandra Microbial Balancing Program Manual

ISBN 0–927978–21–0

2 4 6 8 9 7 5 3 1

*Dedicated to
the stout-hearted ones
who have the guts to plunge
into this program.*

Contents

PERELANDRA MICROBIAL BALANCING PROGRAM MANUAL

Introduction

I had just finished writing the *Perelandra Microbial Balancing Program Manual* when a close friend asked me how I felt about this book and the program. The question caught me a bit off guard because I hadn't stopped to articulate my feelings since getting into the development of the program with nature and then writing the book. The importance of the program seemed self-evident, and putting it into words felt unnecessary. But as soon as my friend asked his question, I realized I had deep feelings.

For me, writing a book and moving it through the production process is similar to birthing a child. I had just finished birthing quite a large child (576 pages) on April 29, 1995, when *Dancing in the Shadows of the Moon* was published. About three months later, I began working with microbial balancing as a new process. As I moved through the writing stage, I had the distinct feeling that I had "gotten pregnant" too soon—my mind and body felt as if they needed more time to recover from the previous pregnancy and birth. But here I was, well along in this new pregnancy and, although I *felt* stretched both mentally and physically, I was surprised to note how exceptionally well I was functioning—physically and mentally. It was as if this child was meant to be, and I was somehow holding together beautifully despite my feelings to the contrary.

Using the birth metaphor, I told my friend that I felt this child was very special. The pregnancy had been a surprise—I certainly had not planned to write a book so soon after *Dancing*—but I felt this child to be tiny, yet extremely powerful. *This* child was going to have a global impact unlike the other Perelandra books. And the other books had already proven to have quite an impact on their own. Why I feel so strongly about this I can't explain—except perhaps to say it is a mother's instinct.

I went on to explain that the Microbial Balancing Program connects humans and nature in a new and intimate way. In this program, human health and balance are achieved by focusing not on the human, but on the health and balance of the vast and vibrant population of living organisms called microbes. Up to now, we have developed a highly adversarial relationship with viruses, fungi, bacteria and protozoa. We control them by killing them. After all, we humans are a lot bigger than they are and killing the "little buggers" should not be an issue for us. In the Microbial Balancing Program, we turn 180 degrees from this thinking and deal with human health issues by cooperating with and ensuring the balance and well being of the "little buggers." We make peace, not war.

For years people who have visited Perelandra for the workshops and open houses have asked me how I "control" the wild animal "problem" in the garden. (The Perelandra garden is right next to a ninety-acre woods, and the fencing around the garden is designed to keep only horses and cows out.) Each time I'm asked the question, I try to get the person to understand that I don't have a problem—nor does my garden—because I changed my attitude. That's all I did. I stopped thinking about and acting toward the wildlife in aggressive ways. They are no longer the enemy. They are welcome in the garden, they may drink from the several water sources we supply in the garden area, and they are welcome to consume ten percent of what the garden produces. It took considerable effort on my part to change my attitude, but the effort was well worth it. We have a regular flow of wildlife that move through the garden area. They stay on the paths and rarely is anything ever eaten, even though they are welcome to eat ten percent of the produce. When I changed my attitude and reflected that change in my actions, how the wildlife interacted with the garden changed. It was clear to me that they no longer felt their survival was in danger and they relaxed. As they calmed down, the population of animals coming into the garden changed, and a new balance was reached.

No matter how much I try to explain this, people invariably look at me as if I'm some drunken alien who just fell out of a spaceship window and landed on my head. They refuse to believe what I am saying. It absolutely cannot be this simple. Surely I have some kind of "special agreement" with nature, and the animals conduct themselves in the garden in light of this agreement. There is no agreement—I just stopped threatening them and began looking at them as part of the appropriate makeup of a garden: They belong. Literally, I could feel that as I changed my attitude, how I physically moved in the garden also changed. I walked differently. I was moving without an air of aggression. It was clear that *I* was the one who created the aggressive air in the garden in the first place, and nature responded naturally and in kind. And by changing my attitude, I created a very different garden environment. Once again, nature responded naturally and in kind. Instead of an environment of survival, we now had one of balanced, respectful coexistence.

Sometimes I am asked how I can remain so calm about the global devastation that is going on right now. Well, I explain that I don't like it any better than the next environmentally-friendly person, but I know something from my many years of working with nature that always brings a little smile to my face: No matter what, no matter how much of the planet we humans destroy, nature will *always* have the final say. We may think we can get the upper hand on nature, but this is only an egotistical illusion on our part. We will never have the upper hand because just when we think we have it, we will have destroyed ourselves and our healthful way of life that much more. Every time we "kill" nature—in the name of control, of course—we kill a part of ourselves. It's easy for some to say I'm exaggerating when I say these things, but I know I am not. In the "war" we humans wage against nature, I know who is going to win. The quality of our entire life on this planet depends on nature. What we breathe, what we drink, what we eat, the materials we use for our structures, our warmth, our cooling, what we wear... even the so-called artificial or synthetic products we use like plastic are created from natural elements—oxygen, hydrogen and carbon—that have only been combined in ways that are not found in nature. Why am I calm about all of this from nature's perspective? Nature does not need us for its existence. But we need nature if we are to exist. I am absolutely certain that in the end, short of our having blown the planet to smithereens, we may become extinct, but nature will have survived us, and it will begin its task of repairing and rebalancing without us. We will only have succeeded in destroying ourselves.

This brings me back to the Perelandra Microbial Balancing Program. In the 1940s and 1950s, researchers made medical history by discovering and developing an extensive array of antibiotics. It was an important time of medical discovery and many lives have been saved as a result. However, it has proven to be a temporary measure as far as our health is concerned. It is now fifty years later—and antibiotics have not made infectious diseases history. In a recent magazine article, scientists listed the major health issues that face us in the twenty-first century. One was "The War Against Bacteria," and they wrote how only deadly new, resistant strains of bacteria have survived the enormous quantities of antibiotics that have been used over the past fifty years. They ended by stating that "controlling the spread of these new bacteria will be crucial for public health in the next century."

In my mind, I see the Microbial Balancing Program making a full circle back to the medical discoveries of the 1940s and 1950s and allowing us humans to try it again. This time, instead of attempting to dominate and control viruses, fungi, bacteria and protozoa, we can use cooperation and care. We can change our attitude and how we approach our relationship with microbes. After all, they belong. As a result of our changes, we can turn infectious disease on its ear.

I looked at my friend with tears in my eyes after talking about all these things because I knew that, although I never would have consciously chosen to get pregnant so quickly after the birth of my previous book, this present book had to be born—and its time was now.

Chapter 1

Perelandra Microbial Balancing Program

Generally, when we are faced with an infection or an infectious disease, our primary concern is to eliminate the microbe causing the problem. We tend to focus on eradicating the cause so the problem can be solved and health can be restored. For most of us, the problem with this thinking is that it does not take into consideration that the cause of the problem—microbes—are a population of live organisms that operate within the laws of nature. The development of drug resistance, which is receiving considerable attention, is only one way that the laws of nature are involved in the interrelationship of microbes and humans. Drug resistance occurs because microorganisms resist any effort to eradicate or kill them. When under siege, they shift into a survival mode because they function within the laws of nature—when attacked, nature does what it must to survive. The weak individuals perish and the strong survive. When bacteria are impacted by antibiotics, they respond by neutralizing the adverse effect of the antibiotic. They do this by mutating. In the short term, most bacteria causing an infection "lose the battle," but the surviving bacteria "win the war." Then the antibiotic no longer threatens their existence. To accomplish this, the bacteria have done nothing more than operate within the laws of nature.

For almost twenty years, I have been working with nature to learn what is required to create a balanced environment within a defined "biosphere." At Perelandra the main focus of this work is the garden. As part of this balancing work, I have had to address the health and well-being of vast and varied populations of microbes (microscopic organisms). They are in the air and soil, and in and on plant systems. Nature has made it clear to me that within any defined biosphere (such as a garden) a balanced microbial population supports that biosphere and enhances its strength. *An imbalance in the biosphere* will affect the microbes and cause a shift within that population that will enable it to adapt to *the imbalance of the biosphere.* Conversely, *an imbalance within the microbial population* will affect the biosphere and force it to shift in order to support *the microbial imbalance.* Another way of saying this is that the microbial imbalance forces the biosphere to be redefined in a way that accommodates the microbial imbalance. From the perspective of the microbes, they now live in an "appropriately balanced environment." From the perspective of the biosphere, there is now weakness reflecting the microbial imbalance. This usually shows up in specific plants that now have diseases caused by viruses, fungi (pronounced: fun' jï) and bacteria.

There are three ways to address these interrelated imbalances. One way is to focus on the environment and attempt to restore it to an appropriate balance. This will cause the microbes to shift to accommodate the changed environmental balance. The second way is to focus on the microbes: Address the balance problems in the microbial population, assist that population as we assist the environment to shift to its appropriate balance, and the environment will adjust. The third way is to focus on both the environmental balance *and* the microbial balance—looking at the problem from both ends. When dealing with environmental and microbial balance, each of these three options for addressing interrelated imbalances must be considered and the appropriate one chosen for the specific situation being addressed.

What does all this about gardens have to do with human infectious diseases? Nature defines a "garden" as follows:

A garden is any environment that is initiated by humans, given its purpose and direction by humans, and maintained with the help of humans. For nature to consider something to be a garden, we must see humans actively involved in all three of these areas. It is the human who calls for a garden to exist. Once the call is made, nature responds accordingly to support that defined call because a garden exists through the use of form.

Humans tend to look at gardens as an expression of nature. Nature looks at gardens as an expression of humans. They are initiated, defined and maintained by humans. When humans dominate all aspects and elements in the life of the garden, we consider this environment to be human-dominant. We consider an environment to be "nature friendly" when humans understand that the elements used to create gardens are form and operate best under the laws of nature, and when humans have the best intentions of trying to cooperate with what they understand these laws to be. When humans understand that nature is a full partner in the design and operation of that environment—and act on this knowledge—we consider the environment to be actively moving toward a balance between involution (nature) and evolution (human).

*As a result, this co-creative environment supports and adds to the overall health and balance of all it comprises **and** the larger whole. It also functions within the prevailing laws of nature (the laws of form) that govern all form on the planet and in its universe. In short, when a garden operates in a balance between involution and evolution, it is in step with the overall operating dynamics of the whole: The various parts that comprise a garden operate optimally, and the garden as a whole operates optimally.*

Nature does not consider the cultivation of a plot of land as the criteria for a garden. Nature considers a garden to exist wherever humans define, initiate and interact with form to create a specialized environment. This is the underlying intent of a garden and the reason behind the development of specialized environments such as vegetable gardens. Nature applies the word "garden" to any environment that meets these criteria. It does not have to be growing in soil. It only needs to be an environment that is defined, initiated and appropriately maintained by humans.

The human body is a garden. It is a biosphere that is defined and initiated by the human soul, and it is maintained by humans on both the conscious and unconscious levels. The physical body itself is the biosphere (or form) that is supplied by nature. The health of this biosphere depends on the state of balance and interaction among all elements that make up what is defined as the human being. Microbes are part of those elements. Without them the human biosphere could not function or survive. They are vital to how the body functions. Eliminating them does not shift the body to a greater state of health. Rather, it shifts it to a vastly weakened and endangered state.

There are five major microbial situations that can cause problems for the body biosphere:

1. One microbe enters the human body and causes one infectious disease such as AIDS *or* TB.

2. Two different microbes enter the human body and cause two infectious diseases simultaneously such as AIDS *and* TB. In this case, AIDS makes the human more susceptible to TB.

3. Many kinds of microbes are released into the body. This occurs when, for example, the appendix ruptures and microorganisms from the intestines are released into the peritoneal cavity.

4. A mixed population of microbes that are a natural part of the body biosphere (such as in the nasopharyngeal area—the throat—and intestinal tract) become imbalanced.

5. A mixed population of microbes on the surface of the body (such as the arm pits) becomes imbalanced.

As in the Perelandra garden, the key to approaching and working with microbes within and on the human body is balance. The ideal state between an invading microbe, the microbes that are a natural part of the biosphere and its host environment or biosphere is *balance*. When an equilibrium between these three elements is maintained, a new natural balance is created and the body does not manifest disease. To obtain this equilibrium, addressing the body directly is not always enough. The balance of the microbes and their relationship to the body's environment need to be considered as well. The Perelandra Microbial Balancing Program was designed by nature to do just this. It applies the principles and processes that have been used successfully in one garden (the Perelandra garden) to the human body garden. And it focuses on one specific, important element within that garden—microbes.

This program may be used in many situations. Obviously, it is to be used any time our health is compromised by a microbial infection. This would include all infections caused by viruses, fungi, bacteria and protozoa. You do not need to know which microbe is causing the infection to use this program. In fact, even if you have been diagnosed by a physician, don't assume the diagnosis is correct. How many times have we heard a physician say, "Well, it's an infection . . . I think it's probably caused by a virus." Translated freely, this means it looks like it could be an infection and the physician has no idea what's causing it. In the Microbial Balancing Program, nature easily identifies the imbalance. They're experts at this kind of thing.

In working with this program for myself, I have discovered that I needed it for things that I would not have associated with microbes. For example: I was feeling especially sluggish and my muscles were stiff. I tested that I needed to do the Microbial Balancing Program for the microbes that were related to this problem. Despite my not understanding the logic behind this, I worked with the program anyway. By the next day I was feeling dramatically better, and by the second day I had more energy and flexibility than I had experienced in months. This example—plus numerous other issues I have tested—has shown me that, except for well-defined infections, we really don't understand how microbial imbalance affects the human body. So I recommend that you automatically test for the Microbial Balancing Program for *any* health-related issue. Don't assume anything. If it's not needed, you will find out that it is not needed. Then you can move on to other health alternatives for dealing with the problem.

If you have no obvious health-related issue to test, you may use the Microbial Balancing Program to *generally balance* the microbes that are a part of your body environment (body biosphere). For a general balancing, you will treat the body's entire microbial population as one interactive unit in terms of the relationship of this unit to the body environment. The purpose of this check is to prevent imbalance. By doing a general balancing once a month, you are able to monitor the state of your microbial balance and respond appropriately if it is beginning to reflect a problem. This is especially important during these times when breakdown of the global environment is having an adverse effect on all life systems.

The microbial population within your body is not just affected by your body's state of balance. It is also influenced by the larger environment outside the body. We are quite aware of the effect the larger environment has on the balance and well-being of our bodies. And it makes sense that whatever affects the body also affects the microbial population. What we don't realize is that the larger environment beyond our body environment also *directly affects* the microbial population. All we have to do is look at the current worldwide outbreak of bacterial, fungal, viral and protozoan diseases in the environment and inside humans to appreciate what I am describing. We are not living in environmentally-friendly times. Using the Microbial Balancing Program as a preventive measure gives you a vital tool for getting through such times while maintaining a state of balance.

AN IMPORTANT POINT: When a biosphere is balanced, it maintains appropriate activity and interaction among all the parts that constitute the biosphere. It naturally and automatically repels anything that does not correspond with or enhance the balance of all that is in the biosphere. This is natural law, and it is also the source of stability and strength inherent in balance. When a biosphere is out of balance, it weakens and becomes vulnerable to and even serves as a magnet for outside elements that support the imbalance. The more a person maintains balance within his body environment, including balance among microbes, the more he will be able to move through life without attracting viruses, fungi, bacteria and protozoa that are currently causing so many serious diseases.

ABOUT WORKING WITH
THE MICROBIAL BALANCING PROGRAM

We are quite used to addressing health-related issues by focusing on ourselves. In effect, we ask ourselves what is "wrong" with our body and/or mind that is causing this specific problem. In short, we humans remain in the center position. In terms of the Microbial Balancing Program, the human body is the "host environment" in which the microbes live. This program is focused on the microbes and the state of the host environment (the body environment) as it relates to the microbes. It is the microbes that take center position. For those who have already used the program, this concept was their first eye-opening experience with it. They had to remind themselves often, especially in the beginning, that all of the testing was for what the *microbes* needed—not what they (the humans) needed. So be aware that you will most likely be faced with this conceptual shift in the beginning. Don't be afraid to remind yourself often that testing is for the microbes.

IMPORTANT: If you have a serious infection, do not refuse needed medical treatment. The Microbial Balancing Program is to be done *in conjunction with* needed medical treatment and not in place of it. If you are on medication, it is important to monitor your microbial balance while taking the medication and after completing the dosage series. I do not suggest you stop taking medication. I assume that if you are taking something, you have a problem that is serious enough to warrant your taking it. However, in order to accomplish one goal, a lot of medication wreaks havoc on many elements in the body. It is important—*especially* when taking something like an antibiotic—to monitor and assist microbial balance so that you don't create more problems in an effort to eliminate the one problem. (Information on how to approach this testing is included in Chapter 3.)

Sometimes when working with the program, you will experience physical reactions. If you test that you need the Microbial Balancing Program, it means that your microbes are not in balance. This program shifts the microbes and the body environment—as it relates to the microbes—back into balance. This, in turn, affects you personally. For example, you may have a sudden dull headache or mild abdominal pains/cramps that last for five minutes. You might also feel a little light-headed or queasy. Or you might have a sudden flair-up of zits or a bout of itching. A couple of people who had poison ivy several weeks prior to working with the program had a mild recurrence of the rash. In each case the reaction/release was mild, and most reactions disappeared within twenty-four to forty-eight hours. A positive way of looking at this is to realize that whatever is being released would remain within you if you did not use the program. The last thing you want is to incubate a microbial problem in your body. Such an imbalance could lead to serious illness in the future.

IMPORTANT

The Microbial Balancing Program has been carefully developed to address the full range of issues with microbes and how they interact within different environments. The program Steps and the steps within the individual processes have been carefully set up with great attention given to the many details that are part of a complex program such as this. For example, when making an essence solution for microbes and their environment, you will add 3 drops of the needed essences to a half-ounce solution bottle. When making an essence solution for yourself, you will add 5 drops of the needed essences to a half-ounce solution bottle. To ensure the quality of the Microbial Balancing Program, the program Steps and process steps must be followed *exactly* as they are written. In the above example, you cannot get sloppy and do essence testing for yourself, using the steps as they are set up for microbes, and expect quality results. This program is easy to do and easy to follow if you "follow the bouncing ball" and don't attempt to rearrange it to suit your own liking.

Also, be sure to tell anyone who is interested in working with the Microbial Balancing Program that it is *vital* that they have a copy of this manual to work from. It is also crucial that they follow the instructions as written in this manual and ignore anyone else's interpretation of what is written. In short, to maintain the integrity of the program always get your information from the *Perelandra Microbial Balancing Program Manual.*

Chapter 2

The Setup

The keys to the Microbial Balancing Program (MBP) are the coning and the chart. The testing for the program is done within a coning, and it is the coning that supplies you with all the information you need for microbial balancing. (The specific information about the Microbial Balancing Program coning will be explained later in this chapter. If you are not familiar with the concept of conings in general, see Appendix D.) The MBP chart functions as the organizing tool for the program. It moves you through the program step by step, and it tells you exactly what to do and in what order you are to do it. All the program's Steps are listed on the chart, so no Steps will be missed when you do the work. Actually, once you learn how to use the chart, you'll realize that it makes doing the program easy. (NOTE: I am capitalizing "step" when it refers to the Steps on the chart. When I refer to steps within individual processes, I do not capitalize the word. I think this will help you to know what step I am referring to.)

As you read this chapter and Chapter 3, I recommend that you have a copy of the chart in front of you to refer to. (NOTE: There are copies of the chart in the back.* Be sure to keep one copy clean for photocopying. And when you have it photocopied, I suggest you get at least fifty copies made. When you experience what this program can do for you, you'll want to use it a lot.) I also suggest that you read Chapters 2 and 3 *thoroughly* before

* The charts may be removed by carefully cutting along the margin with scissors or a razor blade. If you do not wish to remove the charts from this book, you may purchase copies of the chart from us. For ordering information, see the order form in the back of the book.

working with the program—perhaps even twice. This will help you to become familiar with the program and learn where to locate information for quick reference. In general, Chapter 2 contains basic information and insight about each Step of the chart, plus general advice to help you as you learn to use the program. Chapter 3 contains just the process steps you'll be needing when you do the microbial balancing work. This way you won't have to plow through extraneous information to find these steps.

The wide margins in this manual may be used for note-taking. You may also want to highlight or underline key points to refer to later. Unless you have a photographic memory, you will be using the manual every time you do the Microbial Balancing Program. So customize the manual for easy use. For example, you may wish to tab the different process pages in Chapter 3 so that the steps for the specific processes will be at your fingertips— so to speak.

You will be using a new chart every time you do the program, and you will be doing a lot of writing on it. Recording all the test results not only helps you get through the program Steps, it also gives you a record of the microbial work you've done for each issue. I suggest you keep your charts. At some point down the road, you may wish to refer back to them to look for a history of treatment or a pattern of work done for a specific issue.

In order to do the testing that is required in the program, you must know how to do kinesiology. This is an easy muscle-testing technique that enables you to discern "yes" and "no" responses. To make things simple, all the information you need for the program is set up in a yes/no format. *The yes/no is projected to you by the members of the coning.* You discern those answers by doing kinesiology testing. The steps for doing kinesiology are in Appendix A. If you don't already know how to do this testing method, relax: *Everyone* is capable of doing it. Your biggest stumbling block will be your disbelief that something this simple can actually work. (If you already use a pendulum and you are confident in your ability to discern "yes" and "no" with it, it's fine to continue using it for the Microbial Balancing Program. The pendulum is another form of kinesiology.)

You will also need all five sets of the Perelandra Essences—Rose, Garden, Rose II, Nature Program and Soul Ray—and you will need the Expanded Balancing Process Kit. Information about what the essences and the kit are and how they function in the Microbial Balancing Program can be found in Appendices B and C. In general, both the essences and the kit are used for the balancing and stabilizing needs of your microbes, your body environment and yourself that occur during the program testing. (Ordering information for these items is included in Appendices B, C and the order form in the back of this manual.) You will also need to provide a regular dinner tablespoon, some paper towels for cleaning said spoon, a current calendar and a watch or clock with a second hand. While waiting for your essences and Expanded Balancing Process Kit to arrive, you can work on that kinesiology. This way, as soon as you get your package, you can start working with the program. There's only one other thing you will need for doing this program—the burning desire to learn something new.

And this brings me to one other point about the Microbial Balancing Program. I seriously doubt if you have ever dealt with anything like this program before. Some of its concepts will be new to you, and its approach and how it is designed will certainly be new to you, so I urge you to be patient with yourself. This is actually an easy program. (Stop laughing. It is!) Unfortunately, the big hump in the learning curve is right up front. This means you'll be going through a period of time where things will feel klunky, unfamiliar, uncomfortable, and it will seem like it's taking you forever to get through the Steps. These are all the natural results of that learning curve. This program is worth the effort it's going to take you—so besides being patient, you may also need perseverance and a healthy dose of humor. Don't hesitate to laugh at your mistakes, and every once in a while stand back and have a good chuckle over this crazy thing you are learning. Trust me—once you have gone through the chart two or three times, you'll begin to feel confidence creeping in. And by the time you've gone through the chart four or five times, you're going to feel some real comfort: you're becoming an old hand at doing the program.

STEP-BY-STEP INFORMATION ABOUT THE CHART

The First Line

Subject: *Infection from cut on left hand*   Date: 6/25/95

If there are others around you who are doing the program, you may wish to include your initials in the "Subject" space so that you'll be able to easily identify your charts.

1. Devas of the Microbial Balancing Program, Viruses, Fungi, Bacteria, Protozoa, Healing, Pan, WB Connection, Your H.S.

Step 1 lists the members of the Microbial Balancing Program coning. It is to be activated every time you are doing any testing or follow-up work for the program. It is a balanced coning between nature (the involution dynamic) and the human soul (the evolution dynamic) and should not be altered in any way unless you are specifically instructed to do so in this manual in several of the program's processes.

The devic level in the coning is represented by the Deva of the Microbial Balancing Program, which holds the architectural patterns of the program itself, plus the devas of viruses, fungi, bacteria and protozoa (the four major microbial groups), which maintain the architectural patterns of the internal structure of these specific microbes and their life-cycle rhythms. The Deva of Healing, also known as the Deva of Human Healing, is a part of the coning so that the human healing process will automatically be synchronized with any work that is done with the microbes. This deva also functions as an architectural force and creates the physical dynamic and framework found within all human healing. The order, organization and life vitality of the human body—that is, the full physical structure and how it functions—fall within the domain of the Deva of Healing.

Pan is the member of the coning representing the nature spirit level because he is the only nature spirit intelligence that does not have regional limitations. He is universal in dynamic. This means that everyone, no matter where they are positioned on the planet, can work with Pan—and his universality is critical for a program that is intended to be global. In the Microbial Balancing Program, Pan's presence ensures that the devic blueprints for the program itself and the microbes are accurately translated into the appropriate information and action. (By the way, Pan is actually without, or beyond, gender. I refer to him as "him" because his energy feels masculine to me during our communications.)

The White Brotherhood (WB) is a large group of highly evolved souls dedicated to assisting the evolutionary process of moving universal reality, principles, laws and patterns through all planes and levels of form. They hold the major patterning and rhythms now being utilized for the shift we are all going through from the Piscean to the Aquarian era.* When we link with them, as in this coning, they support and assist us by ensuring that

The Piscean era explored, developed and worked with the dynamics of parent/child, higher/lower and masculine-energy-dominant relationships; these dynamics were expressed in both action and structure throughout all levels of form reality.

The Aquarian era into which we are moving emphasizes the concepts of balance, teamwork and partnership. These dynamics will be emphasized in the pattern and rhythm of all life behavior.

any work we do maintains its forward evolutionary motion and its connection to the new Aquarian dynamics. In the Microbial Balancing Program coning, we connect with the White Brotherhood by stating: "I would like to be connected to the appropriate members of the White Brotherhood for the Microbial Balancing Program." Once said, the proper connection will be immediately made.*

"Your h.s." is the chart shorthand for your higher self. This is the final connection in the Microbial Balancing Program coning, and it ensures that whatever work is done in the coning is harmonious and consistent with our soul rhythms and patterns. In short, with our higher selves in the coning, the program cannot compromise who we are and what we are to do.

You don't have to understand a coning in order to open the Microbial Balancing Program coning. All you have to do is go through step 1 (below) and the coning automatically opens. (For your convenience, I have repeated these steps for opening the MBP coning in Chapter 3.) Then you can proceed with the rest of the Steps in the chart. If you want to know more about conings, see Appendix D.

One last point about this coning: Do not remove anyone from the coning list or add others who are not part of the Microbial Balancing Program unless you are specifically instructed to do so in the process steps given in this manual. This is the coning that has been specifically set up for this program. If you alter the coning, its members will consider the work nullified and will simply wait in a holding pattern until you close the coning down. A non–Microbial Balancing Program coning will not function within the Microbial Balancing Program.

* *If you wish to know more about the White Brotherhood, there is additional information in the following books:* MAP: The Co-Creative White Brotherhood Medical Assistance Program *and the* Perelandra Garden Workbook.

Remember, all of the steps for any of the processes you'll need are included in Chapter 3 so that you'll have them located in one place when you are working the program and the chart.

Opening the Microbial Balancing Program Coning

1. State (aloud or to yourself): "I would like to open a Microbial Balancing Program coning." Ask to be connected with the following:

> The Deva of the Microbial Balancing Program (Either wait 10 seconds for the connection or use kinesiology to verify the connection.)
>
> The Deva of Viruses (Wait 10 seconds or verify.)
>
> The Deva of Fungi (Wait 10 seconds or verify.)
>
> The Deva of Bacteria (Wait 10 seconds or verify.)
>
> The Deva of Protozoa (Wait 10 seconds or verify.)

The Deva of Healing (Wait 10 seconds or verify.)

Pan (Wait 10 seconds or verify.)

The appropriate connection with the White Brotherhood for the Microbial Balancing Program (Wait 10 seconds or verify.)

Your higher self (Wait 10 seconds or verify.)

Wait another 10 to 15 seconds to adjust to the coning.

2. In order to ensure your stability in the coning, test yourself for essences (the Basic Essence Test for Humans in Chapter 3) and take any essences that you need. Do not test for dosage. These essences will be taken one time only. Record whatever essences tested positive for Step 1 on the back of the chart.

NOTE: The essence testing for Steps 1, 7 and 9 are directed to you *personally* and not to the microbes or their host environment. For these three Steps—and only these three Steps—you may include in your testing any "non-Perelandra" essences that you have included in your personal health regimen. For all the other Steps, only the Perelandra Essences are to be tested.

The coning is now open, you are stabilized and ready to begin.

2. Identify/Describe Issue

Step 2 sets the focus for you and the coning. It is important that you fully describe the issue you wish to focus on without limiting the focus. For example: You have an itchy rash all over your back. The rash has never been officially diagnosed, but you're pretty sure it is shingles. In Step 2 do not write "shingles." Instead, write "itchy, red rash on back." If the rash is mostly on your back with a few blotches on your left arm and right thigh, write "itchy, red rash on back, left arm and right thigh." Your self-diagnosis (shingles) may be wrong, and when used in this work it will limit the direction and intent of the testing focus. Even if you know what the diagnosis is, don't just use a single name to identify or describe an issue. Instead, write "cold: sneezing, runny nose, coughing, chills in chest area."

If you do not have any specific issues to work on, you may wish to do a *general balancing*. This focuses on the state of the microbial balance in your body environment and shores up weaknesses that may have led to problems in the future, had they been left unchecked. The Microbial Balancing Program recommends that a general balancing be done monthly.* For this work, you only need to write "general balancing" at Step 2.

3. Intent

The intent for the Microbial Balancing Program is determined by you. Steps 2 and 3 join you and the coning in a single, well-defined direction with an equally well-defined purpose. All you have to do is read the sentence: "I request that the coning focus be directed to all VFBP (viruses, fungi, bacteria and protozoa) that impact, are related to or are connected with the above-stated condition or issue."

4. Do These Microbes Need Balancing?

Just because you have identified a problem, set a focus and activated an intent does not mean that the Microbial Balancing Program is what is needed to properly address the situation. In Step 4 you find out if you are to continue. Ask: "Do these microbes need balancing?" Then do a kinesiology test. If the answer is "yes," continue with the chart.

If the answer is "no," you need go no further. As far as this issue is concerned, at this particular time, the microbes are balanced and not causing a problem. Close the coning (Step 9) and find out what you are to do for yourself to address the situation. The Perelandra Organizing Process and chart can be useful. (See Appendix E.) Once you have addressed the problem from *your* perspective, it would be good to do a Microbial Balancing Program check on this issue by opening the coning and again doing Steps 1 through 4. Sometimes the microbial balance cannot be addressed until you have first done some balancing work for yourself. By using the Perelandra Organizing Process chart, you can discern precisely how you are to approach an issue and what is to be addressed in what order.

5. Microbes Being Tested

Step 5 identifies which microbial groups are being worked with and how you are to approach the testing. The implied question you are asking for the first five boxes is: "Regarding the stated issue in Step 2, are _____ in need of balancing?" Whatever tests positive is what the coning is indicating is in need of balancing for this situation.

Do not attempt to determine intellectually which microbes are in need of balancing. For example, even if we know for certain that athlete's foot is caused by fungi, the coning may indicate that bacteria and viruses, not fungi, are in need of balancing for your athlete's foot. And, in case it flairs up again, you may find out when you test that just bacteria in that area are in need of balancing. In short, whatever microbes test positive are the ones in need, despite what we think we know.

"Other" refers to any microbes that are not covered in the VFBP categories. For this work, their devic information is held by the Deva of the Microbial Balancing Program. "Other" also ensures that the microbes that reside in our body environment and have yet to be medically or scientifically identified can be worked with in the Microbial Balancing Program.

In the last two boxes in Step 5, you determine how you are to approach the testing. If you have checked the box for more than one microbial group and you test positive for "test as a unit," you will be continuing through the rest of the Steps just one time. This is because these groups of microbes are being considered one large group to be worked with as a single unit. If you test positive for "tested and treated separately," you will need a chart for each group of microbes that tested positive. For example, you tested positive for testing and treating viruses and bacteria separately. You will now need two charts, each filled out identically in Steps 1 through 4. One chart will deal with the viruses only, so in Step 5 check "viruses." The other chart will focus on the bacteria. Work through Steps 6 through 8 on each chart separately. (How to set up the testing for multiple charts is described on p. 23.) Once you have finished working with the viruses and the bacteria, you may close the program coning. (Even though you are working with two charts, you are still only in one coning, so you will need to close that coning just once.) This multiple-chart approach occurs when each microbial group needs to be approached independently. The work done with each one will complement and support the other. In this case, balance cannot be achieved if the viruses and bacteria have been treated the same and in one unit.

Sometimes—not often—both treatment boxes will test positive. In this case, you are to work with the microbes independently of one another (using a separate chart for each of the microbe groups that test positive), and then use an additional chart to work with them as a unit. *Always work with them independently first* (and in the order they are to be worked), then

follow-up with the unit testing. All of this may seem tedious to even consider, but it's important to remember that this is an area of life's reality—
microbes—that are demonstrating tremendous imbalance as a result of our
attempts to kill them off and the overall breakdown of the larger environment. Sometimes it's going to take a little work on our part to restore
balance. Remember, you may be focusing your attention on a bunch of
microbes while doing this program, but the results of the work are ultimately for your overall benefit—and the results can be enormous.

6. Troubleshooting List

Step 6 is where you get down to business. You have opened the coning,
set the focus for the work, stated the intent, determined if the program is
useful for this focus, discovered which microbes you will be working with
and how you are to approach the work. The Troubleshooting List tells you
what processes you will be using and in what order they are to be done.

For those of you who are used to applying the principles in the *Perelandra Garden Workbooks* to your garden and land work, you will feel like
you are just working another garden. The principles for establishing microbial balance in an environment such as a vegetable garden are the same as
those in a body environment. And the processes used for achieving microbial balance in the garden are what are needed for restoring balance in
your body. In short, the principles and processes remain the same—only
the environment has changed.

IMPORTANT: The process steps as they are written in the *Perelandra
Garden Workbook* and the *Perelandra Garden Workbook II* have been spe-
cially worded and modified here for this program. Because of the unique
setup of the Microbial Balancing Program and the way it functions within
the MBP coning, there are some steps listed in the *Workbooks* that are not
needed for this program. So, to save yourself time and effort, be sure to
use the MBP's steps that are in Chapter 3. However, if you wish to do the
processes for regular garden or land balancing work outside the MBP, you
must refer to the steps as they are written in the *Workbooks*.

One thing that is easy about working these processes within the Microbial Balancing Program is that you don't need to open and close individual
conings for each process in Step 6 as you would when working the processes out of the *Workbooks*. You already have the program coning open,

and all the work done in the program is done under the umbrella of this coning. All you have to do is the process work itself. When finished with one process, just move on to the next one, if another is needed. If a modification in the coning is required for a specific process, that will be listed right in the steps. (This is the only time you are to modify the coning, but do it only as indicated in the process steps in Chapter 3.) For a couple of the processes, you will need to include one additional deva in the coning. This is simple. Request that the deva listed in the steps join the coning, and at the end of the process you will be instructed to ask that deva to disconnect from the coning. *You do not need to close the whole coning down just to disconnect from one member.*

Use the Troubleshooting List to determine the processes that are needed by the microbes. Read each process name on the Troubleshooting List, one at a time, and test using kinesiology. The processes that test positive are the ones that are needed. As you are testing the list, the implied question is: "Is _____ (process) needed for this work?" You need not ask the entire question for each process on the list. Just read down the list and know that when you say "Energy Cleansing Process," you are implying "Is the Energy Cleansing Process needed for this work?" Place a small check beside the processes that test positive.

If more than one process tests positive, you will need to find out in what order they are to be done. These processes work in conjunction with one another and it is important that they be done in the proper sequence. To find out the order, ask the question: "Which process is to be done first?" Then read through the list of the ones that are checked. The process that now tests positive is to be done first. Mark "1" in the blank to the left of the process name. Ask the question again for the process that is to be done second and repeat the testing of the remaining processes you are to do. Repeat this until each process has been assigned a sequence number. Your list may look like this:

4. Energy Cleansing Process
1. Balancing and Stabilizing Process
3. Atmospheric Balancing Process
2. Genetic Balancing Process

This means you are to do the four processes in the following order:

1. Balancing and Stabilizing Process
2. Genetic Balancing Process
3. Atmospheric Balancing Process
4. Energy Cleansing Process

In the above list, you will turn to the Balancing and Stabilizing Process section in Chapter 3. Do the steps exactly as written. When you have completed this, turn to the Genetic Balancing Process section and do those steps as written. Then you will turn to the Atmospheric Balancing Process, and after that you will finish with the Energy Cleansing Process. After you have completed these four processes, pat yourself on the back and move on to Step 7.

IMPORTANT: The processes are to be done one right after another. If you have tested the Troubleshooting List and found that you are to do 8 of the processes, and you don't have time to do all of them at that moment, you can stop right there. Close the coning (Step 9) and return to this chart *within the next 48 hours*. Reopen the coning and read aloud Steps 2, 3 and 5. This reestablishes the focus and intent for the work. You will not need to retest Step 6 for what processes are needed. However, you now need to find out what order you are to do them in. Once you have this information, proceed with the process testing and, when Step 6 is completed, continue with Steps 7 through 9. If you forgot that you were scheduled to leave on a two-week trip to Hawaii the next day and you missed the 48-hour deadline, you will need to start the whole process over on a new chart. This is because variables may come into play after 48 hours that can impact the microbes and change what is needed for the focus you wish to test.

If, for example, in Step 5 "test and treat separately" tested positive for viruses, bacteria and fungi, this means you are now working with three charts. Don't panic. At Step 6, test for which of the charts is to be worked with first, second and third. Then, focusing your attention on the chart to be worked with first, test which processes in Step 6 are needed. Do these processes one after the other. You can use the "scheduling" approach described in the above paragraph if you need to allot more time for doing all of the processes on this chart. *Within 24 hours* after you have completed Step 9 on this first chart, turn your attention to the second chart and do the testing just as you did for the first chart. Go on to the third chart within 24 hours after completing Step 9 on the second chart. NOTE: You may be taking essence solutions for several days as a result of the work you did with chart #1. (Taking essence solutions is explained in the section in this chapter titled "Essences Process for Microbes and Their Environment.") Do not wait for solution dosages to end before starting charts #2 or #3. Wait no longer than 24 hours before starting the next chart. In this situation, essence solution dosages from one chart may be taken while working with and testing another chart. Once testing for all three charts is complete, you may be taking essence solutions for the work done with each.

Under "Bal" and "Stab," record what you used for balancers and stabilizers after each process is done. When working the Essences Process, you will be recording the essences that test positive on the solution line ("Sol") and how many days and how many times a day you are to administer this solution on the "Dosage" line. If you run out of line space, just continue recording the information on the back of the chart.

The following is a brief description of each process listed in Step 6, its focus in relationship to the Microbial Balancing Program and any additional information that you will need—other than the actual steps, which are listed in Chapter 3.

NOTE: To understand these processes in greater depth, I urge you to read the information provided for them in the *Perelandra Garden Workbook II*. For understanding how to work with nature in general in situations outside the Microbial Balancing Program, I recommend that you read both *Workbook II* and the *Perelandra Garden Workbook*. The information in the two books complements one another and will expand your understanding on the subject.

Energy Cleansing Process

The Energy Cleansing Process is designed to remove stagnant emotional energies and correct environmental imbalances that are out of time and place in the environment that has absorbed them, and move those energies out of that environment and onto the next step of their evolutionary journey toward completion. In the Microbial Balancing Program, this process is done from the perspective of the microbes—that is, the microbes define what energies are out of time and place. The environment in question is their host environment—your body and its surrounding environment. You will note that the process works with not only your body, but also with the

3 feet of space that surrounds it. The body and that space make up what is called the "body environment."

Battle Energy Release Process

This process releases energy that was absorbed and is being held within a specific environment as a result of trauma that was released during an historic battle or war, and the day-to-day battles we face such as divorce, verbal and physical fights, abuse, drive-by shootings, gang wars, drug wars, rape, robberies, antibiotics.... The microbes and the host environment—your body environment—as it relates to microbial balance are the focus in this process. Whatever held energy falls within the broad category of battle will be released appropriately.

Balancing and Stabilizing Process

In the *Workbooks*, this process is referred to as the Soil Balancing and Stabilizing Process because, in a garden context, it is primarily used when working with soil. However, it may be used to balance and stabilize any form. In the MBP, the Balancing and Stabilizing Process is used in two ways: (1) as a process by itself, and (2) as part of most of the other processes on the Troubleshooting List. When used in conjunction with another process, it greatly strengthens, protects and enhances the work that is done by the other process. By itself, it impacts the order and organization of all elements that are affected by the work on their molecular level, which, in turn, enhances the life vitality (action) of those elements.

To do this process, you must have an Expanded Balancing Process Kit, which contains all the balancers that are needed for microbial balancing work. The five sets of Perelandra Essences (Rose, Garden, Rose II, Nature Program and Soul Ray) comprise the stabilizers. The balancers in the Expanded Balancing Process Kit address the molecular structure, strength and building needs of the elements being worked with. The essences stabilize the balancing work that is done and link the process to the microbes' intent, direction and purpose.

A note about working with the Expanded Balancing Process Kit: You will find in the steps that *you are not to take the balancers orally.* Many of the balancers are amendments that are normally added to soil. In the MBP Balancing and Stabilizing Process, Pan shifts the energy of the balancers directly to whatever elements are being worked with. When working with soil, this allows people to balance soil 5 feet or 20 feet below the ground's surface without having to rent a bulldozer. When working with the human body, it enables us to balance microbes and specific areas inside our bodies without having to submit to surgery. In short, working with Pan as set up for this process is efficient beyond belief.

For some, working with Pan in such a direct way may seem outrageous and absurd—even uncomfortable. I can certainly understand these feelings. After all, what I am saying is outrageous and absurd. But I suggest that these feelings be put aside until after you have done the Balancing and Stabilizing Process several times. First of all, you will see that the steps for working with this nature intelligence couldn't be easier. And after you have done the process a few times, you'll see that it gives you extraordinary results. Seeing and feeling the results will get you over any discomfort you might have in the beginning.

FINAL NOTES ABOUT THIS PROCESS: The steps in Chapter 3 for the Balancing and Stabilizing Process are written with the focus on using it as a process by itself. The focus of the shift of the balancers and stabilizers is either for specific microbes or the relationship of the microbes to the body environment. When you are doing this process in conjunction with another process, the focus is on the impact and shift in the microbes and body environment that are a result of that other process.

If the Balancing and Stabilizing Process on the Troubleshooting List tests positive, test to see if your focus is to be (1) for a general balancing and stabilizing for the specific microbes in question, or (2) for the microbes' relationship to the host environment. Sometimes—not often—both will test positive. In that case you are to do the process for each focus. Test for the order in which they are to be done.

Also, the balancers may test positive, but the stabilizers test negative. (Or, the balancers may test negative and the stabilizers test positive.) In this first case, the area/work in question needs only balancing. It is already stabilized, and only balancers need to be shifted.

Atmospheric Balancing Process

When using the Atmospheric Balancing Process for microbes in and around a human, "atmosphere" refers to the 3-foot area of space that surrounds the body. This process is included because the atmospheric area is considered part of the body environment and can impact the balance of any element within that environment—including microbes. One of the unique properties of your body's atmosphere is that it is constantly changing. Every time you move, the atmosphere surrounding you changes because you've shifted locations. Also, because atmosphere can be easily permeated by outside elements—bugs, dust, pollution, pollen, rain—it can change whether you physically move or not. In order to work fully with atmosphere, you must add the Deva of Atmosphere to the Microbial Balancing Program coning. This deva supplies the complex and mutable information regarding your atmosphere in relationship to the focus of the microbial balancing work. Don't panic. As I said earlier, adding the deva to the coning and disconnecting from this deva once the process is complete are included in the steps in Chapter 3.

Essences Process for Microbes and Their Environment

To do this process, you will kinesiology test the five sets of Perelandra Essences. To save time and effort, I have set up the basic essence test steps* so that you will first test one box at a time rather than one bottle at a time. This way, if no essences are needed in the box you are testing, you will get a negative result and can put that box aside and go on to the next box. The essences that test positive for you to use are recorded on the "Sol" (solution) line. For microbial balancing, assume you will be taking *one drop of each essence concentrate* if you are placing drops directly on your tongue. However, it is important that you determine the number of days needed for a solution and how many times a day you are to take it. This information is recorded on the "Dosage" line. If you are administering a solution for more than a couple of days, you may wish to make a half-ounce solution bottle for convenience. For a solution bottle, add *three drops of each essence concentrate* to the mixture.**

ABOUT SOLUTION BOTTLES: Suppose you need to take several essences orally several times a day and you work away from home. Half-ounce dropper bottles with glass droppers may be used for solutions. (Essence solution bottles must have glass droppers.) Make the microbial solution as needed right in the bottle, adding *3 drops* of each essence and filling the rest of the bottle with water. If you are planning to use this

* I am referring to the Basic Essence Test for Microbes and Their Environment that is listed in Chapter 3.

** For those of you who use essences outside the MBP and are accustomed to testing for how many drops of each essence concentrate are needed for a solution, this is good news. MBP half-ounce solutions do not need this kind of detailed testing because the number of drops needed has been predetermined for you.

bottle for more than a couple of days, add one teaspoon of brandy or white distilled vinegar as a preservative before filling with water. (Use more preservative if the essences are to be taken for longer than 2 weeks or are exposed to high temperatures.) Shake the solution bottle lightly. Take one dropperful (about 10 to 12 drops) from the solution bottle for each essence dosage.

A note on the water to be used in these solutions: Spring or untreated water is best. But if this is unavailable, tap water will suffice. You can also put *5 drops* of essence concentrate in a glass with 4 ounces of water and refrigerate the solution. Drink one good sip for each dosage.

If you are sensitive to brandy, you may use distilled white vinegar to preserve your solution. Use the same amount of vinegar as you would brandy for proper preservation.

As always, when taking essences be careful not to touch your mouth with the dropper. If you do, wash the dropper well before placing it back in the bottle.

TO ADMINISTER THE ESSENCES (oral, soak, topical or NS application): Before finding out what essences are needed, test this row of boxes on the chart to determine how you are to administer them. Most of the time you will be taking the essences orally. For this, place one drop of concentrate for each needed essence on your tongue or, if you are to take them several days and it would be more convenient, make a solution bottle and take a dropperful each time. Sometimes, however, you may need to soak an area of your body with the solution. The easiest way to soak something is to make a solution in a half-ounce bottle adding 3 drops of each needed essence to water. (No preservative is needed.) Then soak a sterile gauze pad with this solution and, touching only the edges of the gauze pad with your fingers, lay the pad on the area in question for the time needed. To determine the time needed, ask: "How many minutes do I soak this area?" Then do a sequential count. (See p. 53, "Testing for Dosage.") If, in your sequential count, you test positive for 3 minutes but negative for 4, this means you are to soak the area for 3 minutes (not 4). If the pad starts to dry before the soaking time is up, make up another half-ounce of solution and pour enough over the pad to make it wet again.

If you don't know what area is to be soaked, address your question in the coning and start testing body areas. Whatever tests positive is the target area. For soaking your whole body in a tub of water, first run the water in

NOTE: Have sterile gauze pads on hand for those times when you need to soak an area with essences or administer them topically.

the tub, then ask how many drops of each needed essence you are to add to that amount of water. Don't faint at the idea. You won't need 6,000 drops of each essence. You may get up to 30 or 40. Use the same procedure for douching—first fill the bag with warm water, then test for how many drops of each essence are needed. *NOTE: For microbial balancing you can assume that the same number of drops are needed for each essence.*

Sometimes you will test that you are to apply the essences topically. Make the half-ounce solution as you would for soaking (no preservative is needed), and either pour a little directly onto the area in question or soak a gauze pad and rub it over the area, wetting it well.

"NS application" stands for nature spirit application. Place one drop of concentrate for each essence needed into a spoon. Then work with Pan just as you would for steps 5 and 6 in the Balancing and Stabilizing Process. You will ask Pan to appropriately shift the essences for the focus listed under the Essences Process that tested positive—general solution or solution for specific problem.

FOLLOW-UP ESSENCE TESTING: This is an important part of essence testing that many ignore, but it is just as vital that the essence pattern and rhythm be completed for microbial balancing as it is for human health. The easiest way to explain follow-up testing is to describe it. For example, after doing the basic test for whatever focus tested positive under the Essences Process (general solution or solution for specific problem), you found that you needed to take 6 essences for 3 days, 2 times a day. On the fourth day—the day after the first dosage ended—open a Microbial Balancing Program coning, read Steps 2 and 3 on that chart and retest the same Essences Process focus to find out if a new dosage is needed as a follow-up to the first dosage.* This time you may discover that 2 essences are needed for 2 days, 2 times a day. Once this dosage is completed, open the coning and test that focus again. Keep doing this until you test that no other essences are needed. This means that, regarding this focus, the microbial process for which the essences were needed is now complete.

IMPORTANT: Whenever administering an essence solution for the Microbial Balancing Program, whether it be oral, soaking, topical or a nature spirit application, remember to focus your attention on *what the solution is for* at the time you are administering it. This applies to taking the solution while the coning is open *and* when taking a needed dosage during the days following microbial balancing work. The focus will telegraph the solution

* Essence follow-up testing should be done within 24 hours after the completion of an essence dosage.

appropriately to the microbes. All you need to do to focus is think about the purpose for a solution or state the purpose aloud or to yourself. If you are administering a general solution, the focus is on your microbial population as a whole. An example: If in Step 5 bacteria tested positive, and you must administer a general essence solution, this means that to properly address the bacteria imbalance, an essence solution for the full microbial population is needed. If you are administering a solution for a specific problem, all you need to say is that this solution is for the specific problem in question within your body's microbial population. You need not identify the problem any further because it has already been identified by the coning. The solution will automatically and appropriately shift. Also, remember that you are not taking these essence solutions for yourself—you are taking them for your microbes. (For more understanding about focus and its use as a tool, see Appendix F.)

Microbial Triangulation Process

Often in nature, elements within a specific, defined environment are linked in groups of 3 to create strong, balanced, interrelated triangle units. In a garden, the points of a triangle may be 3 different plants or plant varieties. These 3 points have among them connecting links of energy. In a fully balanced and stabilized triangle, the points and the links are strong.

If Microbial Triangulation tests positive, one or more of the points and/or links of a triangle that is connected with the microbes within your body environment is in need of balancing and/or stabilizing. You do not need to know what the points in a triangle are or identify their location in order to do this process. The coning already has this information. You will

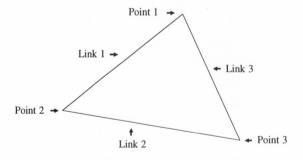

note that on the chart the points and links are identified by number. As soon as you test positive for the Microbial Triangulation Process, the coning "assigns" a specific point and link to each number. Referring to them by number coordinates your focus and work with the coning's focus and work.

To determine which points and links in a triangle you are to work with, ask the following:

"Is the #1 point weak?" (Test.)

"Is the #1 link weak?" (Test.)

Repeat this for the #2 and the #3 points and links. Check the box (or boxes) of whatever tests positive. These are the points and/or links you will be working with.

Sometimes more than one triangle is in need of balancing and/or stabilizing. How to determine this is included in the steps in Chapter 3. If you are working with more than one triangle, set up the testing on the back of the chart for each triangle as follows:

Triangle 2: 1) ☐ point ☐ link   2) ☐ point ☐ link   3) ☐ point ☐ link

     Bal:

     Stab:

Calibration Process

There will be times when the microbes in your body environment will receive an environmental impact that will be so strong that the microbes' form and their devic dynamic will no longer be synchronized. Balancing, stabilizing and triangle balancing will not address this specific situation. The Calibration Process will, and it is simple.

This process is also extremely effective for yourself and land environments. If you are interested in working with the Calibration Process outside the Microbial Balancing Program, see the information on this process in Perelandra Paper #2 or in the books *MAP* and *Workbook II.**

* See the order form in the back of this manual.

Geopathic Zone Balancing Process

Nature defines geopathic zones as being self-contained energy realities found within a defined environment that can either enhance the health, balance and well-being of any life system that comes into contact with them or adversely impact, even destroy, some life systems that are impacted by them.

If geopathic zone balancing tests positive on the chart, this means that within your body environment you have one or more self-contained energy realities that are adversely impacting the microbes in question. If they are to exist and function within the body environment in balance, the geopathic zones need to be neutralized in relationship to the microbes. Our body environment contains numerous self-contained energy realities, and they do not all have an adverse effect on us or our microbes. They are a natural part of any defined environment. The Geopathic Zone Balancing Process is how we can monitor the balance of these realities, thus ensuring that the microbe's balance, and ultimately our balance, is enhanced by them rather than weakened.

This process also requires a modification in the Microbial Balancing Program coning. You will need to add the Deva of Geopathic Zones in order to properly work with all the zones in question. The locations of the geopathic zones do not need to be identified. The Deva of Geopathic Zones supplies this information to the coning. Also, if more than one geopathic zone need balancing, this work will be done simultaneously as you go through all the steps. You will not need to do the process for each zone individually.*

The balancers and stabilizers that you get when doing the testing for this process will cover what is needed for all the geopathic zones that are neutralized. Individual testing for each geopathic zone is not needed.

Genetic Balancing Process

NOTE: This process is not described in any other Perelandra publications at the present time.

For this process, you will be balancing the microbes in question by linking them to the genetic blueprint that is being held by their deva. This link will once again fuse the microbes physically to the dynamics, rhythms, patterns, powers, strengths and balances that are a natural part of that blueprint. Due to various reasons—such as environmental impact or genetic engineering—the links between a physical living organism and its devic blueprint are seriously reduced or compromised. In microbes, one example of this problem is the super bacteria that rapidly develop as a survival response. For some of these bacteria, the resulting mutation is an organism that is different than what has been genetically coded and held within the devic blueprint. The physical structure is now seriously out of sync with its genetic blueprint. If we wish organisms to exist and function within our body environment in a balanced way, they must have strong links with their devic blueprint, and the Genetic Balancing Process can assist in re-establishing those strong links.

Factor-X, Factor-Y and Factor-Z

Factor-x is the coning's way of alerting us that something else needs our attention. In short, factor-x assures us that all the bases are covered, and it allows us to transcend what we intellectually know, understand and/or perceive about microbes, their balance and their relationship within our body environment. "Factor-y" and "factor-z" are indications that more than one factor-x needs to be addressed, and each gets its own name tag. As you test through the alphabet, the coning "assigns" a specific issue to each name tag at the instant you test positive for that letter. When doing the actual work with these various unknowns, the coning knows precisely which issue you are working with because you are referring to it by its agreed-upon name—factor-x or factor-y or factor-z.

If, by chance, you test positive for factor-x, y and z, make sure only 3 unknowns need to be worked with by continuing your testing at the beginning of the alphabet and asking if there is a factor-a. If so, test for a factor-b. Test until you get a negative. Again, don't panic. You won't test positive for factor-a very often.

When determining the order the processes are to be done in Step 6, treat factor-x, y and z as separate processes and not as a unit. For example, if four processes plus factor-x and factor-y are checked on the chart, factor-x may need to be second and factor-y fourth.

Record the balancing and stabilizing information for each factor on the back of the chart.

7. Personal Solution

Kinesiology test Step 7, asking: "Do *I* need a personal solution as a result of the microbial work?" If you get a positive response, it means you need to be stabilized because of the work. To determine which essences are needed, *shift your focus to yourself* and do the Basic Essence Test for Humans that is listed in Chapter 3. (Non-Perelandra essences may be included in the testing in this Step.) Make sure you find out how many days and how many times a day you are to take the solution.* This solution is independent of any solutions you are taking for the microbes, and you

** If you need to make a solution bottle, add **5 drops** of each needed essence to a half-ounce bottle. Then add a teaspoon of brandy or distilled white vinegar if you need to preserve the solution.*

*If you wish to make a solution in a glass, add **9 drops** of each needed essence concentrate to 4 ounces of water. Add 3 teaspoons of brandy or distilled white vinegar to preserve this solution. Refrigerate it if no preservative is added. Drink one good sip for each dosage administered.*

must focus on *your need to stabilize as a result of the microbial work* each time you take your personal solution.

Do follow-up essence testing for yourself just as you would for the essences used for the microbes. Continue the follow-up testing until you no longer need any essences. NOTE: If you are scheduled to do a trouble-shooting recheck (Step 8), and you test for a new personal solution in Step 7 in the recheck, *discontinue taking the previous (original) solution.* Just take the new (recheck) personal solution. If you test negative for a new solution, the original one is still effective and you are to continue taking the original dosage. Be sure to test for follow-up essences for either solution when its dosage is complete.

8. Troubleshooting Recheck Date

* If the recheck includes another Essences Process solution and you are still taking an Essences Process solution as a result of the original testing, discontinue taking the original solution. Replace it with the new recheck Essences Process solution. If you test negative for a new solution, the old one is still effective and you are to continue taking the original dosage. Be sure to test for follow-up essences for whatever solution you take when the dosage is complete. NOTE: If you are working multiple charts for an issue, and the first round of work on chart #1 schedules a recheck even before you start the last of the multiple charts, do that chart #1 recheck in its right timing. Start multiple charts in their 24-hour rhythm no matter what follow-up or rechecks are required for any individual chart.

Sometimes the microbes involved in the focus that was identified in Step 2 may need additional rounds of troubleshooting (Step 6) in order to complete the shifts and changes that are needed. It is necessary to establish a pattern and rhythm of movement. When you get to Step 8 on the chart, ask: "Is a troubleshooting recheck needed?" If you get a negative response, simply continue on to Step 9. If you get a positive response, ask for the date. You may approach this by testing a calendar. The day that tests positive is the date for the recheck. You have up to 48 hours after that date to do the recheck testing if you are to maintain the rhythm of the ongoing work.*

To do the recheck, open a Microbial Balancing Program coning and read Steps 2 and 3. This reestablishes the focus and intent of the testing. Test Step 4. If you get a negative response, the first round of work completed was what was needed after all, and you can close the coning. Consider the issue as stated in Step 2 now clear as far as microbial balancing is concerned. If the response was positive, proceed with Steps 5 through 9 using a clean chart.

If you miss the 48-hour recheck deadline, open a coning and read Steps 2 and 3 to key in focus and intent. Then test Step 4. If more work is needed, continue with the Steps using a clean chart. The work you do may be the original recheck work that was needed or you may have to do that work and an extra process or two. It all depends on what has occurred with the microbes and within your body environment since the time the original rhythm was missed. In short, if you miss the recheck date, you may have a bit more work to do to bring the issue to completion but you will not lose the benefits of the work already done.

9. Close Coning

Closing or dismantling the coning is as easy as activating it.

1. State (aloud or to yourself): "I'd like to close the coning." Ask to be disconnected from:

> The Deva of the Microbial Balancing Program*
>
> The Deva of Viruses
>
> The Deva of Fungi
>
> The Deva of Bacteria
>
> The Deva of Protozoa
>
> The Deva of Healing
>
> Pan
>
> The appropriate connection with the White Brotherhood for the Microbial Balancing Program
>
> Your higher self

* You do not have to wait 10 seconds or verify each member's disconnection. Simply read through the list, clearly stating each member's name.

Wait 10 or 15 seconds for the dismantling to fully occur, or kinesiology test that the coning is now closed. If it is not, you lost your focus during the closing process. Collect yourself and go through step 1 again.

2. Test yourself again for essences to make sure your participation in the coning itself hasn't challenged your balance. (Non-Perelandra essences may be included in this testing.) Take the needed essences *and check for dosage* to see if they are to be taken more than one time. If so, remember to think about what this solution is for each time you take it.

NOTE: In the beginning, while you are getting used to this coning work, you may need more essences and dosages over longer periods of time. Be patient with yourself. These essences are helping you maintain your balance. If you are testing several charts, whether the issues are related or not, you may need a Step 9 solution for each chart. Focus on the intent listed in Step 2 while taking each solution for Step 9.** Also, if you do any recheck work (based on test results in Step 8) and you test for a new solution in Step 9 in the recheck, discontinue taking the previous solution. Just take the new "recheck" solution for Step 9. If you test negative for a new solu-

** This focus will identify the chart and issue for which you are taking each solution.

tion, the old one is still effective and you are to continue taking that dosage. Be sure to test for follow-up essences when the dosage is complete.

IMPORTANT: If you feel hungry once the coning is closed, you may be experiencing a protein drain. Eat protein first, then reward yourself with a piece of good chocolate.

ADDITIONAL POINTS TO REMEMBER

ABOUT YOUR HIGHER SELF: When you disconnect your higher self from a coning, you are not disconnecting it *from yourself*. You are simply shifting the special focus the higher self has maintained in order to function in a coning back to the normal focus that surrounds the connection and relationship you consciously have with your higher self on a day-to-day basis.

ABOUT OPENING AND CLOSING A CONING: The only thing that will interfere with opening and closing a coning is your focus. If you focus on what you are doing and request that a coning be opened, each member of the coning will automatically and instantaneously connect as you state their name. The same is true when closing a coning: As you state each member's name, that member will automatically and instantaneously disconnect. There is never an argument about this. You are in charge of opening and closing conings. No other member of the coning will ever override your responsibility in this. So if you get to this point and you feel the coning doesn't "wish" to close despite the fact that you are requesting it, ignore those thoughts. You're just a little nervous. The Microbial Balancing Program coning isn't made up of a bunch of thugs from a street gang who are waiting to mount a coup. If you are focused on what you are doing and you request that the coning be closed, it will be closed as soon as you read through the list of members to be disconnected. Also, it is important to close the coning once each working session is complete. Leaving a Microbial Balancing Program coning open beyond a testing session will drain your physical energy.*

* If you forget to close a coning, close it as soon as you realize your mistake. Then test yourself for any essences that are needed as a result of your leaving the coning open. You will regain your energy level once the coning is closed.

When you have completed the program testing, you may be taking, for example, a microbial essence solution (Step 6: Essences Process) and a personal solution (Step 7) over the next few days. If you are scheduled to take the two solutions at the same time of the day, *take the microbial-directed solution first*, then take your personal solution.

Although you are to do the processes in Step 6 one right after the other, you may take short breaks (10 to 15 minutes) between the processes in Step 6, as well as between the MBP Steps. However, unless absolutely necessary—such as needing to go to the bathroom—don't take a break *during a process*.

As stated previously, it is possible to integrate this program into your life without creating chaos with your schedule. The problem, of course, is that when testing for microbial balancing you won't know ahead of time how many processes you will need or how long it will take you to move through the testing. For each chart, you need to move through the process testing in Step 6 within one session. I repeat the following approach:

1. Set up and test program Steps 1 through 5. For Step 6 (Troubleshooting List), test what processes are needed. Do not find out what order they are to be done in.

2. Estimate the time you will need for doing the processes that tested positive and arrange for that amount of time *within the next 48 hours.**

3. For the second session; open the Microbial Balancing Program coning, test for essences and read aloud Steps 2, 3 and 5. This reestablishes the focus and intent of the work. You will not need to retest Step 6 for what processes are needed. However, you now need to find out what order you are to do them in. Once you have this information, proceed with Step 6 and, when Step 6 is completed, continue through the remaining Steps.

In this chapter I have tried to cover all the possible situations you might run into while using the program. If you are feeling overwhelmed right about now, this would be a healthy reaction. After all, you've just gotten everything dumped in your lap at one time. But everything doesn't kick in every time you do the program. The actual testing smoothes out and becomes quite manageable. (It now takes me about 20 minutes to test something. It takes the Perelandra staff about 30 minutes to an hour to complete a chart. If we hit a more complex situation, of course the testing will take longer.) If all this has given you a headache and you are thinking about going no further with the Microbial Balancing Program, I urge you to commit yourself to doing the program just 3 times. By that time, you'll start to feel comfortable with the processes and the chart, and you'll also experi-

* *If you miss this deadline, the testing will still give you an idea of the extent of work needed. Estimate the time needed to do the processes that test positive. Then, as soon as you can schedule this block of time, open the coning and begin testing again using a new chart. Although the processes that test positive now may not be the same as what tested positive originally, the list will be about the same, and the time you have allotted will cover the amount of time needed for the testing.*

ence what the program can do for you. Then decide if you'd like to go on or not.

AT LAST, A TRULY HELPFUL SUGGESTION: So you think, even after reading all my suggestions, you'll never find the time to do the Microbial Balancing Program. Here's another suggestion made by a member of my staff: Make an appointment with a doctor to have your infection, illness or chronic problem checked out. Then do the Microbial Balancing Program while you're sitting in the waiting room. It's wasted time anyway, and your only other option is to read six-month-old *Field and Stream* magazines.

MORE ENCOURAGEMENT

I asked members of the Perelandra staff if they had anything about the Microbial Balancing Program they'd like to "say" to the readers of this manual that might be helpful. The following is what they want to pass along. Because they use all of the Perelandra processes, they very quickly wove the Microbial Balancing Program in with everything else. This is why, when writing about microbial balancing, several of the staff also mention the Organizing Process (included in this manual as Appendix E), MAP and MAP/Calibration (for more information, see the book *MAP*). Remember, you do not need to do any other Perelandra process in order to use the Microbial Balancing Program. It is designed to "stand on its own."

I've had remarkable results with the Microbial Balancing Program. Not only has my attitude about bacteria (and microbes in general) changed, but my appointments with the dentist have been reduced from a lot of time in his chair to a couple of visits. It certainly couldn't have come at a better time since I was about to prepare for a microbial battle as the dentist instructed. After reading the manual and balancing the microbes related to the condition, I understood the importance of microbial balancing. This manual has given me the steps to make progress that is continual and fulfilling.

N. W., Washington, Virginia

I usually get one good cold a year somewhere in the early fall, just around the normal weather change from dry summer days to cooler wet days. So I wasn't surprised when, in the middle of October, I started feeling "a cold comin' on." But this time I reacted differently than in past years. Rather than just accept the fact that I was getting a cold and get ready to sneeze and cough my way through it, I got out my Organizing Process chart. I opened the coning and listed the symptoms that I was feeling: stuffy head, scratchy throat, achy sinus and low energy. I then went on to test which processes I needed to do for this issue. I tested positive for the Microbial Balancing Program and a diet change. I tested negative for all the other processes. So I went on to the Microbial Balancing Program chart. I tested that all I needed was an essence solution (six essences) to be taken orally seven times a day for two days.

I made my solution, took one dose and went to bed. By evening of the following day, after taking several doses of my solution, my symptoms were lessening. By the next morning, the cold symptoms were completely gone. I continued my solution through the prescribed time—somewhat in shock that I didn't have to endure two weeks of suffering through a cold.

R. P., Sperryville, Virginia

I had developed pain in an upper molar. When I went to the dentist, he said I would need at least a crown, and possibly a root canal. I was in the chair for three hours while he did extensive drilling and electro-surgery, followed by a temporary crown. I was to return in two weeks to see whether the pain and sensitivity had abated so we could proceed with a permanent crown, or whether the root canal would have to be done first.

After the Novocain wore off, I was in more pain than before. I did not relish the idea of a root canal. So, I checked the Microbial Balancing Program chart to see if anything was needed. The microbial process lasted five days. By the time I went back to the dentist, the pain and sensitivity were gone and I did not need a root canal. He installed the permanent crown and I have been fine since.

I'm convinced the Microbial Balancing Program was the key to successfully completing the crown work without needing further surgery. What struck me the most was a sense that my microbes and I were working together, rather than doing battle with each other. Instead of feeling that something out of control was happening to me, I felt that I had played an important role in my own healing process.

C. W., Jeffersonton, Virginia

Upon showering for work one morning, I was shocked to discover a very tender lump the size of a large lima bean under my left arm. I had never had a lump like this before, and I was quite worried about what it might be, especially given its sudden appearance and unusually large size. Right after the shower, I tested myself for essences and almost all the essences tested positive. This sent me even further down the panic spiral. I called in late for work, opened a MAP coning and spat out my fears and what I was physically experiencing. Feeling a little calmer by the end of the forty minutes, I had the presence of mind to turn to the Organizing Process chart. The first thing that tested positive to do was a microbial balancing.

Right after work that day, I launched into the microbial balancing. It was my second time using the program, and I winced when I tested for virus, fungi, bacteria, protozoa and "other," all to be tested and treated separately. Nevertheless, I went straight into troubleshooting the first category of microbes. As the first chart took shape and I began the actual balancing work, I felt my anxiety over my physical condition give way to a sense of relief and power. Instead of worrying about this unfamiliar and scary problem, I was working to resolve it. The charts proved to be lengthy, one consisting of eight processes in Step 6, with two charts needing recheck dates. The whole process (including seven program charts and lots of essence solutions) took me sixteen days, but after the first three days the lump was significantly smaller and less sensitive. After about ten days, I had practically forgotten about the physical symptom and just focused on following through with essence solutions and chart rechecks. By the time I was finished, I realized what a powerful and effective tool the Microbial Balancing Program is.

C. D., Amissville, Virginia

AUTHOR'S NOTE: Do not hesitate to seek appropriate medical attention for conditions such as this if you would feel more comfortable including traditional support. Perelandra's processes and programs are designed to be used in conjunction with standard medical treatment as well as by themselves. Let your good sense be your guide in making this decision.

During the second week of August, on the way home from work, I realized that the vaguely tired feeling I had that morning had developed into a sore throat, runny nose and sinus pressure. I thought about the various "bugs" that friends had been telling me about that were going around their work places. According to them, I would be miserable for at least a week or two.

I headed for the Organizing Process chart, and tested for a microbial balancing, as well as a MAP/Calibration. Working off of the Microbial Balancing Program chart, I found that my microbes needed just two things—an essence solution and a calibration. Pretty simple. I didn't even need a personal solution, which kind of surprised me. After taking care of the needs of my microbes, I did the MAP/Calibration that night, and the next morning the symptoms were very mild. I went on with life, and in a few days realized I had never gotten sick. The symptoms were completely gone.

It's now fall, and when I hear on the radio that doctors are recommending that everyone get a flu shot for the coming season, I feel very thankful that I have the

Microbial Balancing Program to use. With it my microbes and and I can get along very well.

A. B., Sperryville, Virginia

As a mother of two boys who attend elementary school, I know to expect that quite a few flus and viruses will get passed around from child to child in school during the fall and winter seasons.

One evening my eleven-year-old son came to me looking mighty sad and said that his stomach was not feeling very well. He had begun getting the sniffles the day before and now he was also coughing quite a bit. I realized I needed to get serious about whatever was going on with him, so we sat down together and I began testing him to find out what he needed. When the Microbial Balancing Program tested as the first thing to do, I thought about how I was going to get him comfortable enough to sit through the surrogate testing. *(See Chapter 4 for surrogate testing a child.)* I decided to sit at one end of the sofa and have him lay down with his feet in my lap. I put my essences, Expanded Balancing Process Kit and MBP manual on a table that I pulled in front of me. It worked very well since he wasn't up for much activity and just wanted to snuggle on the sofa anyway.

It turned out that the surrogate testing was pretty painless and I was done within thirty-five minutes. The microbes that needed testing were bacteria and fungi, to be done as a unit. They only needed one process—balancing and stabilizing to my son's body environment. I then tested him for a personal solution that he needed as a result of the Step 6 work, which he was to take for five days, once a day.

He stayed home from school the following day and rested. He was coughing less, his stomach was fine and I could see he was on the mend. He felt good enough to go to school the following day, and it was not long before he was back to his normal, spunky self. And I don't know if the Microbial Balancing Program had anything to do with it, but he did manage to play a great soccer game that weekend, scoring three goals!

It feels wonderful to know I have the Microbial Balancing Program to use for my children. I feel it can benefit them in so many ways, and I am thankful that they can experience the approach to life that is inherent in the program.

S. H., Sperryville, Virginia

Throughout my life, I have been "afflicted" with rashes. As a very young child, my lips suddenly swelled and itched one day, for no apparent reason. By the time my mother got me to the doctor, my ears were red and itchy. Hundreds of questions and many dermatology tests later, no clue. The rash was gone and the doctors determined nothing. A few years later, itchy red patches of rash appeared on my body again. This time, the doctor called it "hives," attributed it to nerves and again, the rash disappeared on its own. Through adolescence, spending lots of time in the woods and around creeks, I experienced the usual bout of poison ivy rashes, which I treated the typical way—with lots of calamine lotion. As a young adult, the "hives" returned on several occasions. Once, I saw a doctor who made some strange and useless diagnosis, gave me Benadryl for the itching and swelling and sent me on my way. After that, I just let the rashes come and go. Until I got the poison ivy rash that wouldn't leave. After three weeks of itching and a rash spreading in the weirdest patterns, I went to a doctor who told me it probably had gotten into my bloodstream and the only way to get rid of it was to take prednisone. So I dutifully followed the two-week prescription and the rash went away. A few years later, in my late twenties, I again began to get what I thought was poison ivy. Instead of the doctor's pills, this time I went for a "natural" solution—the homeopathic remedy made just for poison ivy. The rash spread quickly and I became very ill, experiencing more symptoms than just itching rashes. I got worried, thought I had "shingles" and began my war with this illness. This time, I had a plan. I had just spent several years studying herbal medicine intensively and I knew I could take care of this myself. So I drank gallons of herbal teas, with herbs to take care of each symptom. I made poultices, took herbal baths, changed my diet and got all the right vitamins and minerals to strengthen my immune system. I worked very hard to take control of whatever virus this was that was determined to make me suffer. The symptoms were gone within a week—but only temporarily. For the next year, the rash returned on a regular basis, almost every month. If I caught it in time and drowned myself in "natural remedies," I could stop its progress. I examined every possible reason for this and tried hard to figure out what this illness was about. During this time, I began to work with flower essences and MAP. I addressed my symptoms in detail, at one point taking sixteen different flower essence solutions. Using this approach, I had a year's reprieve from the rash attacks.

This past summer, rashes returned again and again. This time, it gave me the opportunity to make a 180-degree shift in how I approach illness. I had thought that I was taking a different approach all along. I had moved from the conventional doctor's methods to the "natural" and "non-traditional" ways of health care, to balancing my body's electrical system. What more could I do? I received the Microbial Balancing Program just before the summer's second outbreak of rashes. During the first process, my attitude toward the other things that lived in my body began to shift. For the first time, I acknowledged that these viruses and bacteria were actually living organisms that moved and ate and breathed. I had always known that intellectually, but I didn't fully understand what it meant. Now I understand that I can shift health imbalances in my body by focusing on these living organisms—from their point of view. Using the program was much simpler and took less time and effort than all my previous attempts to control my rashes. And this time, it wasn't a matter of control: Finally, I was attempting to shift the balance of my entire internal environment, not just for my sake, but for the sake of all that the environment contained. With this approach, I was truly working from the inside out—for the very first time.

The first time I used the program, it was not for a rash, but I experienced definite changes and symptoms of change happening in my body. Next I used the program on some unidentified "itchy red bump condition" that was different from my other rashes. It looked more like chicken pox than poison ivy. Within days of using the microbial balancing, the bumps subsided and symptoms disappeared. While using the program to address this illness, I began to include the Organizing Process chart. This gave me the structure needed to address my health needs from a number of angles and the insight to address the health of my home environment. As it turned out, I needed to use the Microbial Balancing Program and the garden Troubleshooting Process (*Workbook II*) on my property. Doing all of this took care of the "itchy red bump condition" quickly and painlessly. As I did the processes, I felt I was being much more effective in this approach than I had been before, and the work was more complete, without my feeling I needed to go into battle.

A week after the bumps were gone, the dreaded rash appeared. It started on my eyelid, moved to my ears, then hands and arms and legs. Within two days, I was completely miserable. This was the rash from hell that had me down for a year, and it was back again. I started using the Organizing Process chart immediately. And because my face was swollen beyond recognition, I panicked and went to see a doctor for a diagnosis. The doctor, who was at first determined to discover what this was, ran a long series of blood tests. That was a useless exercise, but a helpful reminder to me. By the time the results of the series of blood tests were all in, all showing nothing, the rash was gone. The once determined doctor told me she didn't have a clue what it was and "if it comes back, see a dermatologist." Sure.

Although the rash was gone within days, it is now three months later, and I continue to work with four Organizing Process charts for the condition. The symptoms being addressed include physical, emotional, mental aspects and several unidentified factors. It becomes clearer and clearer to me that the rashes were just one tiny aspect of something larger going on in my body, something that involves much more than I can presently understand. For the first time in my life, I feel like I have some control where my health is concerned, only because I have stopped battling and given up trying to take control. Now I can feel what "the body is a garden" means. I don't just understand it intellectually. I feel it on every level and the understanding continues to deepen as I approach each health issue with gentleness, moving through the Steps of the charts with a rhythm and structure that simplifies my health concerns and takes the pressure off me personally. I can address issues with a better sense of trust and right timing. I don't have to panic and I can relax with the process.

By integrating the Microbial Balancing Program with the other Perelandra processes, and using the Organizing Process chart, I can feel my health changing from its foundation, rather than from the surface. I am gaining a truer sense of awareness of balance and imbalance, in very real (sometimes gross) ways. Each time I do the Microbial Balancing Program, I experience very physical changes or a release in my body. My face breaks out, I get nauseous, or feel a weird cramp or a headache. None of these things lasts very long nor are they very painful. They come and go quickly. When these symptoms go and I complete the Steps and recheck dates, I feel a marked difference from my "before MBP" health and "after MBP" health. My health doesn't just return to normal, it improves. The process is gradual and feels natural. And the effects definitely feel long term—the solutions are no longer temporary. All aspects of my health are moving and changing together. A new pattern of health and balance is being woven. I am now working with my body and all the little living things contained within it. That has made all the difference in the world.

W. G., Washington, Virginia

Chapter 3

The Steps
for the Processes

The following are the Perelandra processes in the Microbial Balancing Program in the order they are listed on the chart. The steps have been modified to reflect their use for microbial balancing. To do these processes for other situations, do not use these steps per se. Instead, use the steps as listed in the two books, the *Perelandra Garden Workbook* or the *Perelandra Garden Workbook II*. Also, as I have said, if you wish to understand these processes fully, I *strongly* urge you to read the information on each of them in the *Perelandra Garden Workbook II*.

I suggest that you read this chapter several times before working with the program so that you can familiarize yourself with the process steps.

NOTE: Included in this chapter is the information needed for testing while on medication.

ABOUT STEP 6: The Microbial Balancing Program coning that you open in Step 1 is used for all the processes in Step 6. Any needed modifications are noted in the process steps. To do the work, you will need the five sets of Perelandra Essences, the Expanded Balancing Process Kit, a tablespoon, several paper towels and a watch or clock with a second hand.

1. State (aloud or to yourself): "I would like to open a Microbial Balancing Program coning." Ask to be connected with the following:

The Deva of the Microbial Balancing Program (Wait 10 seconds or verify the connection.)

The Deva of Viruses (Wait 10 seconds or verify.)

The Deva of Fungi (Wait 10 seconds or verify.)

The Deva of Bacteria (Wait 10 seconds or verify.)

The Deva of Protozoa (Wait 10 seconds or verify.)

The Deva of Healing (Wait 10 seconds or verify.)

Pan (Wait 10 seconds or verify.)

The appropriate connection with the White Brotherhood for the Microbial Balancing Program (Wait 10 seconds or verify.)

Your higher self (Wait 10 seconds or verify.)

Wait another 10 to 15 seconds to adjust to the coning.

Use the Basic Essence Test for Humans for this testing.

2. To ensure your balance after opening the coning, test yourself for essences* and take any essences that you need. Do not test for dosage. These will be taken one time only. Record the essences you needed.

The coning is now open, you are well stabilized and ready to begin.

ENERGY CLEANSING PROCESS

1. The area to be cleansed is your body—internally and externally. Picture the outline of your body or, if this is difficult for you to do while maintaining focus, place a simple line drawing of a human body (that vaguely resembles yours) in front of you during the process.

2. Prepare yourself for doing the process. Relax and focus.

3. Directing your attention to the coning, state to yourself or aloud:

"I would like to do the Energy Cleansing Process. I ask that what I am about to do be for the highest good, and that I be protected fully during this process."

4. State:

"I ask that any inappropriate, stagnant, darkened or ungrounded energies be released from my body environment. I request this knowing that the cleansing and transmutation process I am about to be a part of is a process of life, of evolution and not negation."

5. Now, shift your focus and visualize the area to be cleansed.

6. Visualize a thin white sheet of light forming 3 feet below your feet if you are sitting in a chair (or beneath you if you are on your back in bed). Allow the outside edges of the sheet to extend 3 feet beyond the widest point of your body's circumference.

7. Ask the members of the Microbial Balancing Program coning to join you as together you slowly move the sheet up and through the area to be cleansed. "Watch" or sense the sheet as it moves. Allow the sheet to rise 3 feet above your head, and then stop.

NOTE: If the sheet moves too slowly or too quickly, or one side is not rising to the same height, ask that the sheet stop; request any changes and then ask that the sheet continue to be raised. The changes you requested will be in place.

8. State that you now wish to create a bundle with the sheet. Visualize or sense the sheet forming a bundle of white light that totally encloses the collected energies. To the left of the bundle, see a gold cord. Tie the bundle closed with this cord.*

9. State:
> "I now release the bundle to the Microbial Balancing Program con-
> ing, so that the energies that have been released can be moved on
> to their next higher level for transmutation and the continuation of
> their own evolutionary process."

Watch the bundle lift. IMPORTANT: *Just watch.* Don't try to determine where the next higher level is.

10. Return your focus to your now-cleansed body. Observe and feel, sense or see any changes.

11. Shift your focus to your breathing, focusing on your body as you inhale and exhale 3 or 4 times.

12. Recognize the members of the coning that assisted you during this process: the devas of the Microbial Balancing Program, Viruses, Fungi, Bacteria, Protozoa and Healing, Pan, the Microbial Balancing Program

* If you do not "see" a gold cord, simply request that the coning help you by tying the bundle closed with a gold cord.

White Brotherhood connection, the white sheet, the gold cord and the energies that were released.

13. Return your focus to your body environment.

14. Balance and stabilize the work that was just completed. Ask:
"What balancers are needed following this energy cleansing?" (Test your Expanded Balancing Process Kit.)

Put one tablet or pour a small amount (about 1/16 teaspoon) of each balancer needed into a spoon. Hold the spoon out in front of you. State: "I ask Pan to appropriately shift these balancers throughout my body environment." Wait 10 seconds for the shift to complete. (Do not introduce the balancers orally.) Record the balancers on the chart.

Then ask:
"What stabilizers are needed following this energy cleansing?" (Test the five sets of Perelandra Essences.)

Take one drop of each needed essence orally. After taking a drop of each, state: "I ask Pan to appropriately shift these stabilizers throughout my body environment." Wait 10 seconds for the shift to complete.

15. If you don't need to do another process for Step 6, refer to Step 7 on the chart for the conclusion of the Microbial Balancing Program.

BATTLE ENERGY RELEASE PROCESS

1. State your intent to do the Battle Energy Release Process and that you come in the spirit of care, concern and co-creativity to help release from your body environment the appropriate battle energies.

2. The release: Ask the members of the coning to now release all the battle energies in question with gentleness and ease, and request that the released energy gather as an energy cloud 3 feet above your head.

NOTE: If at any time you are uncomfortable while an energy release is going on, simply ask that the release occur a little more slowly or gently— or whatever is needed for you to feel comfortable. The members of the coning will immediately comply with your request.

Feel the release, or just wait quietly while the release is going on. This will take anywhere up to 15 minutes. When you sense that the release is complete, kinesiology test to verify or simply wait the full 15 minutes.

3. When the release is complete, request that the released energy that has gathered as an energy cloud over your head now move to its next higher level within the universe. (Do not try to determine where that might be.)

4. Spend a moment noticing the changes and sensations you might be feeling. This serves to fully ground the completed process for you.

5. Balance and stabilize the work you have just completed. Use the same steps you used to balance and stabilize the Energy Cleansing Process (step 14)* or refer to the Balancing and Stabilizing Process. Record the balancers and essences you needed on the chart.

Reword the questions to apply to a battle energy release rather than to an energy cleansing.

6. If you don't need to do another process for Step 6, refer to Step 7 on the chart for the conclusion of the Microbial Balancing Program.

BALANCING AND STABILIZING PROCESS

1. State your intent to do the Balancing and Stabilizing Process for whatever focus has been checked on the chart—as a general balancing for the specific microbes or for the microbes' relationship to the body environment.

2. Ask:
   "What balancers are needed?"
Then test all of the balancers in your Expanded Balancing Process Kit. Ask:
   "Do I need _____?"
Whatever gets a positive response is what is needed.

3. Now ask Pan to assist you. (Pan is already in the coning, but you are focusing on Pan in a special way for this part of the process.)

4. Put one tablet or pour a small amount (about 1/16 teaspoon) of each balancer needed into a tablespoon. Do not take the balancers orally. Hold the spoon out in front of you. State:
   "I ask Pan to receive the energies from these balancers and shift
      them in the appropriate amount for (1) the specific microbes, or (2)
      to my body environment in relationship to its microbes."
Continue holding out the spoon for about 10 seconds, giving ample time

for the shift. Once completed, drop the balancers onto the paper towel. Don't try to save them because they are now form without energy and are no longer useful. Record the balancers on the chart.

5. Turn your attention to the stabilizers—the Perelandra Essences. Ask: "What essences are needed for stabilization?"

Test all of the essences. Whatever tests positive is what is needed.

NOTE: When the "NS application" box on the chart tests positive (Essences Process), you are to administer the essences by doing steps 5 and 6 of the Balancing and Stabilizing Process.

6. After taking one drop of each needed essence orally, state: "I ask Pan to appropriately shift these stabilizers to (1) the specific microbes, or (2) to my body environment in relation to its microbes."

Wait 10 seconds for the shift to occur. Record the essences on the chart.

7. Spend a moment sensing any changes. You do not need to balance and stabilize the Balancing and Stabilizing Process!

8. If you don't need to do another process for Step 6, refer to Step 7 on the chart for the conclusion of the Microbial Balancing Program.

ATMOSPHERIC BALANCING PROCESS

Use the Perelandra Essences as both balancers *and* stabilizers when working with atmosphere. However, you will need your Expanded Balancing Process Kit for a final balancing and stabilizing of your body environment.

1. State that you would like to do the Atmospheric Balancing Process. Then picture/visualize the atmosphere around your body.*

* Visualize the 3-foot area of space that surrounds your body.

2. Include the Deva of Atmosphere in your coning. State: "I would like to include the Deva of Atmosphere in this coning." Wait 10 seconds, then verify the connection. If you test negative, you lost your focus. Regroup, refocus and state your request again. Then test to verify the connection.

3. Ask:
   "What essences are needed for balancing the atmospheric space around my body?" (Test essences.)

Place one drop of each needed essence into the spoon. *Do not take these balancers orally.*

4. Ask Pan to assist you, and then state:
   "I ask Pan to receive the energies from these balancing essences and

shift them appropriately to the atmosphere around my body."
Hold out the essences for about 10 seconds. Clean and dry the spoon.
Record the balancers on the chart.

5. Ask:
"What essences are needed for stabilizing the atmospheric space
around my body?" (Test essences.)
Place one drop of each in the spoon. *Do not take these stabilizers orally.*

6. State:
"I ask Pan to receive the energies from these stabilizing essences
and shift them appropriately to the atmosphere around my body."
Hold out the essences for about 10 seconds. Clean and dry the spoon.
Record the essences on the chart.

7. Check to see if you now need to balance and stabilize your body
environment. (Ask: "Does my body environment now need balancing and
stabilizing?") Since the atmospheric balance has now changed, your body
environment may need a comparable shift in its balance. Doing a regular
balancing/stabilizing will facilitate this. Use the Expanded Balancing Process Kit for balancing and the Perelandra Essences for stabilizing. Shift
whatever is needed as described in the Balancing and Stabilizing Process.

8. Disconnect the Deva of Atmosphere from the coning. State: "I ask
that the Deva of Atmosphere release from the coning." Wait 10 seconds or
verify the disconnection. Again, if you test negative, you lost your focus.
Regroup, refocus and state your request again. Then test to verify the disconnection. This time you'll get a positive.

9. If you don't need to do another process for Step 6, refer to Step 7 on
the chart for the conclusion of the Microbial Balancing Program.

ESSENCES PROCESS FOR MICROBES
AND THEIR ENVIRONMENT

IMPORTANT: Whenever administering an essence solution for the Microbial Balancing Program, remember to focus on what the solution is for at
the time you are administering it. In this process in Step 6, if you are
administering a general solution, the focus is on your microbial population
as a whole. If you are administering a solution for a specific problem, all

you need to say is that this solution is for the specific problem being focused on within your body's microbial population. You need not identify the problem any further because it has already been identified by the coning. Also remember that you are not taking these solutions for yourself—*you are taking them for your microbes.*

Basic Essence Test for Microbes and Their Environment

1. Test to determine whether you are doing a general solution and/or a solution for a specific problem. Check the appropriate line on the chart. Then state your intent to essence test for whatever tests positive. If both tested positive, do one test at a time. *Test the specific problem first and administer those essences, then test the general solution and administer those essences.* Focus your intent appropriately each time. (If you are testing essences as part of the balancing and stabilizing of another process in Step 6, you do not need to state an intent. The intent for the test is already established for that process.)

Also, test how you are to administer the essences and check the appropriate box.*

2. Place each *box* of essences, one at a time, in your lap. Ask: "Are any essences from this box needed for the microbes?"

If you get a negative, you don't have to test the bottles from that box because none are needed.

If you test positive, test each bottle from that box individually to determine which ones are needed. Ask: "Is _____ essence needed?"

HINT: For the box of essences in dram-size bottles that includes several rows of essences, test the bottles *one row at a time* by looking directly at each row and asking if any essences are needed from row # ___. You don't need to test the individual bottles for the rows that test negative. By testing one box or row at a time, the amount of testing can be dramatically reduced.

3. Check your results by placing in your lap just the bottles that tested positive. Ask:

"Are these the only essences needed?" (Test.)
If the response is positive, go to step 4.**
If you get a negative, retest the other essences. A negative means you

missed an essence and need to find what was missed. After retesting, ask the question once more.

"Are these the only essences needed?" (Test.)

If the response is still negative, keep testing the essences until you get a positive response to the question.* This will verify that you have all the essences required for the process.

4. If you have more than one essence, check them as a combination by placing all of them in your lap and asking:

"Is this the combination needed?" (Test.)

If you get a negative even though the essences tested positive when tested individually, you may need to adjust the combination. This means that when the individual essences that tested positive were put together, a combination was created that made one or more of those essences unnecessary. The whole was stronger and more effective than the sum of its parts. Just test each of the combination bottles separately by asking:

"Do I remove this bottle from the combination?" (Test.)

Whatever tests positive gets removed. Then put the remaining combination bottles in your lap and ask:

"Is this combination now correct?" (Test.)

You should get a positive. If you don't, test the *original* combination again, and keep working at it until they test positive as a unit.

5. Focus and administer the essences as directed: oral, soak,** topical, NS application. Remember, you are administering them for the microbes and your body environment that the microbes interact with. Record the essences on the chart.

Testing for Dosage

Find out how many days or weeks you are to administer the essences that are needed. *NOTE: When essences are used as part of balancing and stabilizing, you do not need to test for dosage. They are to be administered one time only—at the time you are doing the balancing and stabilizing.*

1. Hold in your lap all the bottles that tested positive as a unit.

2. Ask if the essences are needed more than one time. If negative, that means, "No, they don't need to be administered more than one time," and you have already completed the dosage part in the above step 5.

* If your kinesiology is "breaking down" and you keep testing negative (and it looks as if you'll never get out of this step), you need to back away from the testing and take a short break. You are nervous, distracted and/or tired. If you are tired, take a short break and decide if you should continue the testing or if you should close the coning and rest. When you open the coning again, start the testing from the beginning and use a new chart. If you are distracted, take a short break, do what you need to do to eliminate the distraction and return to the testing where you left off. If you are nervous, take a short break, regroup, give yourself a pep talk and relax, Then return to the testing where you left off.

** For soaking: Do a sequential test to find out how many minutes you are to soak. Ask if you should soak:
"1 minute?" (Test.)
"2 minutes?" (Test.)
And so on, until you get a negative. Your last positive will tell you how many minutes are needed. Record the time on the chart.

3. If positive, find out how many days you should administer them and how many times per day. Do a *sequential test*. With the needed essences in your lap, ask yourself:

"Are these needed one day?" (Test.)

"2 days?" (Test.)

"3 days?" (Test.)

Do a count until you get a negative response. If you need to administer the essences for 3 days, you will test positive when you ask, "1 day?", "2 days?", "3 days?" When you ask, "4 days?" you will test negative. That will tell you that the microbes would be assisted and strengthened by having the essences available for 3 days, not 4 days.

Daily Dosage

Using the same format, ask if they should be administered:

"1 time daily?" (Test.)

"2 times daily?" (Test.)

And so on, until you get a negative. Your last positive will tell you how many times per day they are needed. Record the dosage on the chart.

Make a solution bottle (3 drops of each essence per half-ounce bottle) if it is to be taken more than a couple of days or if you need to take it several times throughout the day and must carry the solution around. Take one dropperful (about 10 drops) for each dosage.*

Generally, essences are to be administered in the morning and/or in the evening and/or in the mid-afternoon. If you wish to be more precise, test to see if it is best to administer them in the morning, afternoon or evening, or any combination of the three.

Remember to do the follow-up testing once the dosage for each solution is completed. (See Chapter 2, p. 29.)

MICROBIAL TRIANGULATION PROCESS

1. State that you wish to do the Microbial Triangulation Process.

2. Identify which point(s) and/or link(s) of a triangle are involved by focusing on each of the boxes on the chart, one at a time, and asking:

"Does the point/link for # ___ need balancing? (Test.) Does it need stabilizing?" (Test.)

* Add a teaspoon of brandy or distilled white vinegar if you need to preserve the solution, and fill with spring or untreated water. If this is unavailable, tap water will do. You can also refrigerate the solution, thus eliminating the need for preserving it with brandy or vinegar. NOTE: If you wish to make a solution in a glass, add 5 drops of each needed essence concentrate to 4 ounces of water. Add 3 teaspoons of brandy or distilled white vinegar to preserve this solution. Refrigerate the solution if no preservative is added. Drink one good sip for each dosage administered.

Record your test results. Whatever tests positive is a weak spot.

3. You will do a balancing and stabilizing for each weak point and/or link. For each weak point/link ask:

"What balancers are needed?" (Test your Expanded Balancing Process Kit.)

Record your test results.

After asking Pan for assistance, place a small amount of each balancer needed into the spoon, and request that Pan shift the energy appropriately to the point or link you are working with. Use the same process to work with Pan as you would in the Balancing and Stabilizing Process. Then ask:

"What stabilizers are needed?" (Test the Perelandra Essences.)

Record your test results.

After taking one drop of each needed essence orally, ask Pan to shift the entire solution from your mouth to the point/link you are working with.

NOTE: Do both the balancing *and* stabilizing for each weak point or link before addressing the next weak point or link. Don't balance all the weak points and links, then go back and stabilize all of them.

4. Once the work for this first triangle is complete, ask if there is another triangle you need to work with. If so, repeat steps 2 and 3 for each triangle in need of balancing and/or stabilizing.*

* Set up testing and record any additional triangle information on the back of the chart.

5. If you don't need to do another process for Step 6, refer to Step 7 on the chart for the conclusion of the Microbial Balancing Program.

CALIBRATION PROCESS

1. State your intent to do a Calibration Process. Then ask Pan for assistance. (Although already in the coning, you will need to "alert" Pan of your intention to initiate the Calibration Process since Pan does the actual calibration.)

2. State:

"I ask that the microbes in question be calibrated with their devic dynamic, and I ask, with Pan's assistance, that this be done now."

3. Wait quietly for 10 minutes for the calibration to occur. After 10 minutes, verify that the process is complete. If you get a "no," wait another 2 minutes. This time it will be complete, and you don't need to verify it.

4. Test for needed balancers (use the Expanded Balancing Process Kit). With your focus on the microbes that have just gone through the calibration, shift the balancers exactly as you would with Pan for the Balancing and Stabilizing Process. Record the balancers needed on the chart.

5. Test for needed stabilizers (use the Perelandra Essences). Again focus on the microbes that have just been calibrated and, after taking one drop of each needed essence orally, shift the essences with Pan to the microbes in question. Record the essences needed on the chart.

6. If you don't need to do another process for Step 6, refer to Step 7 on the chart for the conclusion of the Microbial Balancing Program.

GEOPATHIC ZONE BALANCING PROCESS

1. State your intent to do the Geopathic Zone Balancing Process, then include the Deva of Geopathic Zones in the coning. State: "I would like to include the Deva of Geopathic Zones in this coning." Wait 10 seconds, then verify the connection.

If you test negative, you lost your focus. Refocus and state your request again. Then test to verify the connection again. This time you'll get a positive. NOTE: *The focus for this process is your body environment.*

DO THE ENERGY CLEANSING PROCESS

1. The area to be cleansed is your body—internally and externally. Picture the outline of your body or, if this is difficult for you to do while maintaining focus, place a simple line drawing of a human body (that vaguely resembles yours) in front of you during the process.

2. Prepare yourself for doing the process. Relax and focus.

3. Directing your attention to the coning, state to yourself or aloud:
   "I would like to do the Energy Cleansing Process for geopathic zone balancing. I ask that what I am about to do be for the highest good, and that I be protected fully during this process."

4. State:
   "I ask that any inappropriate, stagnant, darkened or ungrounded energies be released from the geopathic zones within my body

environment. I request this knowing that the cleansing and transmutation process I am about to be a part of is a process of life, of evolution and not negation."

5. Now, shift your focus and visualize the area to be cleansed.

6. Visualize a thin white sheet of light forming 3 feet below your feet. Allow the outside edges of the sheet to extend 3 feet beyond the widest point of your body's circumference.

7. Ask that the members of the MBP coning for the Geopathic Zone Balancing Process join you as together you slowly move the sheet up and through the area to be cleansed. "Watch" or sense the sheet as it moves. Allow the sheet to rise 3 feet above your head, and then stop.

NOTE: If the sheet moves too slowly or too quickly, or one side is not rising to the same height, ask that the sheet stop; request any changes and then ask that the sheet continue to be raised. The changes you requested will be in place.

8. State that you now wish to create a bundle with the sheet. Visualize or sense the sheet forming a bundle of white light that totally encloses the collected energies. To the left of the bundle, see a gold cord. Tie the bundle closed with this cord.*

9. State:

> "I now release the bundle to this Microbial Balancing Program coning, so that the energies that have been released can be moved on to their next higher level for transmutation and the continuation of their own evolutionary process.

Watch the bundle lift. IMPORTANT: *Just watch.* Don't try to determine where the next higher level is.

10. Return your focus to your body. Observe or sense any changes.

11. Shift your focus to your breathing, focusing on your body as you inhale and exhale 3 or 4 times. This will help ground you and the process.

12. Recognize the members of the coning that assisted you during this process: the devas of the Microbial Balancing Program, Viruses, Fungi, Bacteria, Protozoa, Healing and Geopathic Zones, Pan, the Microbial Balancing Program White Brotherhood connection, the white sheet, the gold

If you do not "see" a gold cord, simply request that the coning help you by tying the bundle closed with a gold cord.

cord and the energies that were released.

13. Return your focus to your body environment.

14. Balance and stabilize the work that was just completed in this process. Ask:

"What balancers are needed for this geopathic zone energy cleansing?" (Test your Expanded Balancing Process Kit.)

Put one tablet or pour about 1/16 teaspoon of each balancer needed into a spoon. Hold the spoon out in front of you. State: "I ask Pan to appropriately shift these balancers to the geopathic zones in question. Wait 10 seconds for the shift to complete. Record the balancers on the chart.

Then ask:

"What stabilizers are needed for this geopathic zone energy cleansing?" (Test the Perelandra Essences.)

You may take any needed essences orally—one drop of concentrate. After taking a drop of each of these essences, state: "I ask Pan to appropriately shift these stabilizers to the geopathic zones in question." Wait 10 seconds for the shift to complete.

DO THE BATTLE ENERGY RELEASE PROCESS

1. State your intent to do the Battle Energy Release Process for the Geopathic Zone Balancing Process and that you come in the spirit of caring, concern and co-creativity to help release from your body environment any held battle energies.

2. The release: Ask the members of the coning to now release all the battle energies held within the geopathic zones with gentleness and ease, and request that the released energy gather as an energy cloud 3 feet above your head.

NOTE: If at any time you are uncomfortable while an energy release is going on, simply ask that the release occur a little more slowly or gently—or whatever is needed for you to feel comfortable. The members of the coning will immediately comply with your request.

Feel the release, or just wait quietly while the release is going on. This will take anywhere up to 15 minutes. When you sense that the release is complete, kinesiology test to verify or simply wait the full 15 minutes.

3. When the release is complete, request that the released energy that

has gathered as an energy cloud over your head now move to its next higher level within the universe. (Do not try to determine where that might be.)

4. Spend a moment noticing the changes and sensations you might be feeling. This serves to fully ground the completed process for you.

5. Balance and stabilize the work you have just completed. Use the same steps you used when balancing and stabilizing in the Energy Cleansing Process (step 14)* or refer to the Balancing and Stabilizing Process. Record the balancers and essences you needed on the chart.

Reword the questions to apply to this battle energy release for geopathic zones rather than to an energy cleansing.

DO THE BALANCING AND STABILIZING PROCESS

1. State your intent to do the Balancing and Stabilizing Process for the Geopathic Zone Balancing Process.

2. Ask:
    "What balancers are needed?"
Then test all of the balancers in your Expanded Balancing Process Kit. Ask:
    "Do I need _____?"
Whatever gets a positive response is what is needed.

3. Now ask Pan to assist you. (Pan is already in the coning, but you are focusing on Pan in a special way for this part of the process.)

4. Put one tablet or pour a small amount (about 1/16 teaspoon) of each balancer needed into a spoon. Do not take the balancers orally. Hold the spoon out in front of you. State:
    "I ask Pan to receive the energies from these balancers and shift
        them in the appropriate amount for (1) the specific microbes or (2)
        my body's geopathic zones in relationship to its microbes."
Continue holding out the spoon for about 10 seconds, giving ample time for the shift. Once completed, drop the balancers onto the paper towel. Don't try to save them because they are now form without energy and are no longer useful. Record the balancers on the chart.

5. Turn your attention to the stabilizers—the Perelandra Essences. Ask:
    "What essences are needed for stabilization?"
Test all of the essences. Whatever tests positive is what is needed.

6. After taking one drop of each needed essence orally, state: "I ask Pan to appropriately shift these stabilizers (1) to the specific microbes, or (2) to my body's geopathic zones in relation to its microbes."

Wait 10 seconds for the shift to occur. Record the essences on the chart.

7. Spend a moment sensing any changes. You do not need to balance and stabilize the Balancing and Stabilizing Process.

The Geopathic Zone Balancing Process is complete.* Pat yourself on the back and disconnect the Deva of Geopathic Zones from the coning. State: "I ask that the Deva of Geopathic Zones release from the coning." Wait 10 seconds, then verify. If you test negative, refocus and state your request again. Then verify the disconnection. This time you will get a positive. If you don't need to do another process for Step 6, refer to Step 7 on the chart for the conclusion of the Microbial Balancing Program.

* The Geopathic Zone Balancing Process includes the Energy Cleansing Process, the Battle Energy Release Process and the Balancing and Stabilizing Process. You may need to repeat any of these three processes in Step 6 if they test positive on their own. For example, you may need to do an Energy Cleansing Process, then do it again as part of the Geopathic Zone Balancing Process. You need to repeat it because the focus for one is different than the focus for the other. One energy cleanses the body environment as a unit. The other shifts the focus and energy cleanses specific geopathic zones in a specialized way.

GENETIC BALANCING PROCESS

1. State that you wish to do a Genetic Balancing Process.

2. Working with Pan (focus your attention on Pan in the coning), ask that the microbes in question be linked to the genetic blueprint being held by their deva. Wait 10 seconds for this link to occur.

3. Request that the genetic blueprint be fused with the microbes on their physical genetic level. Wait 2 minutes for the fusion to complete.

4. Test the microbes in question for any balancers (Expanded Balancing Process Kit) that are needed as a result of this genetic fusion. Focus your intent on the microbes that have just been fused, and shift the needed balancers exactly as you would with Pan for the Balancing and Stabilizing Process.**

** See step 5 in the Balancing and Stabilizing Process.

5. Test for stabilizer needs (the Perelandra Essences). Again focus your intent on the microbes that have just been fused and shift the needed essences with Pan.*** Record the essences on the chart.

*** See step 6 in the Balancing and Stabilizing Process.

6. If you don't need to do another process for Step 6, refer to Step 7 on the chart for the conclusion of the Microbial Balancing Program.

FACTOR-X, FACTOR-Y AND FACTOR-Z

For each factor, do the following:

1. State your intent to work with factor-___.

2. Wait quietly for 7 minutes while the coning does the work needed for this specific issue. No additional time will be needed for this work, so you need not verify that the work is complete at the end of 7 minutes.

3. After 7 minutes, do the Balancing and Stabilizing Process for this factor. This balances and stabilizes the work that has just been completed.

4. If you don't need to do another process for Step 6, refer to Step 7 on the chart for the conclusion of the Microbial Balancing Program.

BASIC ESSENCE TEST FOR HUMANS

This process is not listed specifically on the chart. However, you will use it for Steps 1, 7 and 9 whenever testing yourself.

1. State your intent to do a basic essence test for any essences that are needed *by you* as a result of the coning or the work that has been done.

2. Place each box of essences, one at a time, in your lap. Ask: "Do I need any essences from this box?"
If you get a negative, you don't have to test the bottles from that box because none are needed.
If you test positive, test each bottle from that box individually by placing the bottle in your lap to determine which ones are needed. Ask: "Do I need ____ essence?"
HINT: Test the bottles in the dram box of essences one row at a time.

3. Check your results by placing in your lap just the bottles that tested positive. Ask:
   "Are these the only essences I need?" (Test.)
If the response is positive, go to step 4.*
If you get a negative, retest the other essences. A negative means you missed an essence and need to find what was missed. After retesting, ask the question once more.
   "Are these the only essences I need?" (Test.)

* *If only one essence is needed, skip step 4 and go to step 5.*

If the response is still negative, keep testing the essences until you get a positive response to the question. This will verify that you have all the essences required for that specific Step.

4. If you have more than one essence, check them as a combination by placing all of them in your lap and asking:

"Is this the combination I need?" (Test.)

If you get a negative even though the essences tested positive when tested individually, you may need to adjust the combination. This means that when the individual essences that tested positive were put together, a combination was created that made one or more of those essences unnecessary. The whole was stronger and more effective than the sum of its parts. Just test each of the combination bottles separately by asking:

"Do I remove this bottle from the combination?" (Test.)

Whatever tests positive gets removed. Then put the remaining combination bottles in your lap and ask:

"Is this combination now correct?" (Test.)

You should get a positive. If you don't, test the *original* combination again, and keep working at it until they test positive as a unit.

5. Take these essences orally, one drop each. Remember, this solution is *for you*. To better understand your process, it is helpful to read the definitions for the essences that you need. Record the essences on the chart.

Testing for Dosage

1. Hold in your lap all the bottles that tested positive as a unit.

2. Ask if you need the essence(s) more than one time. If negative, that means you have already completed the dosage in the above step 5.

3. If positive, find out how many days you should take them and how many times per day. Do a sequential test. With the needed essence(s) in your lap, ask yourself:

"Do I need these one day?" (Test.)

"2 days?" (Test.)

"3 days?" (Test.)

Do a count until you get a negative response. If you need to take the essences for 3 days, you will test positive when you ask, "1 day?", "2 days?", "3 days?" When you ask, "4 days?" you will test negative. That will tell you that you will be assisted and strengthened by having the essences available for 3 days, not 4 days.

Daily Dosage

Using the same format, ask if you should take the essences:

"1 time daily?" (Test.)

"2 times daily?" (Test.)

And so on, until you get a negative. Your last positive will tell you how many times per day they are needed. Record the dosage on the chart.

Generally, essences are to be administered first thing in the morning and/or last thing in the evening and/or in the mid-afternoon. If you wish to be more precise, test to see if it is best to administer them in the morning, afternoon or evening, or any combination of the three.

Don't forget that non-Perelandra essences may be included in the personal essence testing done in Steps 1, 7 and 9.

Make a solution bottle if the solution is to be taken more than a couple of days or if you need to take it several times throughout the day and must carry the solution around. Because you are a human and not a microbe, you will need to add *5 drops* of each essence needed to the half-ounce bottle. Then add a teaspoon of brandy or distilled white vinegar if you need to preserve the solution, and fill with spring or untreated water. If this is unavailable, tap water will do. You can also refrigerate the solution, thus eliminating the need for preserving it with brandy or vinegar. Take one dropperful (about 10 drops) for each dosage. If you wish to make a solution in a glass, add *9 drops* of each needed essence concentrate to 4 ounces of water. Add 3 teaspoons of brandy or distilled white vinegar if you want to preserve this solution. Refrigerate it if no preservative is added. Drink one good sip for each dosage needed.

Remember to do all the needed follow-up testing. (See Chapter 2, p. 29.)

CLOSE CONING

1. State (aloud or to yourself): "I'd like to close the coning." Ask to be disconnected from:

The Deva of the Microbial Balancing Program

The Deva of Viruses

The Deva of Fungi

The Deva of Bacteria

The Deva of Protozoa

The Deva of Healing

Pan

The appropriate connection with the White Brotherhood for the Microbial Balancing Program

Your higher self

Wait 10 or 15 seconds for the coning to dismantle, or kinesiology test that the coning is now closed. If it is not, you lost your focus during the closing process. Collect yourself and go through step 1 again.

Remember, if you are focused on what you are doing and you request the coning to be closed, *it will be closed as soon as you read through the list of members to be disconnected.*

2. Check *yourself* again for essences using the Basic Essence Test for Humans to make sure that your participation in the coning hasn't challenged your balance. Take those essences and *test for dosage* to see if they need to be taken more than one time. Remember to think about what this solution is for each time you take it. Record the essences and dosage on the chart, and remember to do any needed follow-up testing. (p. 29)

If you need to make a solution bottle, add *5 drops* of each essence needed to a half-ounce bottle and preserve it as is done for the personal solution in Step 7. If you wish to make a solution in a glass, add *9 drops* of each needed essence concentrate to 4 ounces of water. Add 3 teaspoons of brandy or distilled white vinegar to preserve this solution. Refrigerate the solution if no preservative is added. Drink one good sip for each dosage needed.

MICROBIAL TESTING
WHILE TAKING MEDICATION

While taking medication, check for general balance once a week. This will be in addition to any microbial balancing work that is needed because of the specific problem for which you are taking the medication. One focus will be on the microbial balance as it relates to the specific problem or issue, and the second focus will be on general microbial balance as a result of the impact of the medication. Treat both focuses independently and use a separate chart for each.

When you have stopped taking the medication, check once again for general balance and do all the needed follow-up work. This ensures that the microbial balance has been fully restored.

Chapter 4

Surrogate Testing for Microbial Balancing

Once you experience the results of using the Microbial Balancing Program for yourself, I feel you will want to help those around you who are having health difficulties and could benefit from microbial balancing. As you have probably figured out by now, this is not something that is likely to be offered as part of mainstream medicine. For those illnesses and problems such as colds or flu where one often seeks over-the-counter comfort, microbial balancing may be just what a person needs. It may also be just the thing someone needs to stop the cycle of getting multiple colds or flu each season. For serious illnesses requiring mainstream medical attention, it is important that a person be supported in the healing process by using alternative approaches such as the Microbial Balancing Program *in conjunction with* the necessary mainstream work.

It is really quite easy to surrogate test another person—adult or child— for the Microbial Balancing Program using a simple kinesiology method that is based on the method you have been using to test yourself. In surrogate testing, you link with the other person's electrical system and read all the test answers through your own system. Your two electrical systems are "plugged" into one another and this allows the other person's electrical responses to impact your system, thus enabling you to kinesiology test using your fingers but reading his responses.

The key to making sure you are reading the other person's responses and not your own is step 1 (below) of the Surrogate Testing Process. *You must first clear yourself for any essences that you might need so that your electrical system is fully balanced as far as the Microbial Balancing Program is concerned.* If you do not clear yourself first, whatever essences you need and whatever part of your electrical system is not in balance will "bleed" into the surrogate testing, and your electrical system will respond, altering the test results. If your electrical system is cleared first, it will not override the surrogate test or be a factor in the test results. You will get clean and clear answers from the person you are testing. So don't get sloppy about step 1. The integrity of the rest of the testing depends on it.

IMPORTANT: I recommend that you use the Microbial Balancing Program for yourself and get comfortable with the processes and testing before you surrogate test someone else. I have written this chapter assuming you have already worked with the program on yourself and are comfortable with it. Some points that are explained in the earlier chapters are not repeated in this one.

Also, it is important for the integrity of the testing and the program itself, plus for the support of the person, that you *always* be physically present with anyone you are working with. Do not try to do this program with someone long-distance. It is not appropriate and it will not work.

SURROGATE TESTING PROCESS

1. SETUP: Always clear yourself just before testing another person. State aloud or to yourself: "I would like to prepare myself for surrogate testing the Microbial Balancing Program." Then do a basic essence test for yourself and take any needed essences. You do not need to test for dosage. These will be taken one time only.

NOTE: At Perelandra, we urge people to use the flower essences that are right for them. So, if you have non-Perelandra sets on hand, feel free to use them for surrogate testing the MBP Steps 1, 7 and 9—the Steps that focus on the person directly. *However, for the other Steps in the program, you will need to use only the five sets of Perelandra Essences.*

2. Physically make contact with the person you are going to test and remain physically connected throughout all the surrogate testing on the chart. Have him* place a hand on your knee or touch your foot with his foot. Focus on the person for a few seconds. This *touching and focusing* connects his electrical system to yours. Test your connection using the kinesiology technique, asking (aloud or to yourself) if you are fully connected to this person's electrical system. If negative, spend a few more seconds focusing on the individual—and make sure you are physically touching. If either of you is being distracted, move to a quieter room or quiet the environment you are in. Encourage the person to keep his mind focused on the testing or on the hand (or foot) that is touching you. A wandering mind will cause fuzzy test results. Test your connection again.

3. If the test for your connection to the other person was positive, you are ready to surrogate test the Microbial Balancing Program. Using a new chart, write the person's name, a short description of the issue being tested and the date on line one.

Surrogate Testing the Chart

Step 1: Open the coning and include both your higher self *and* the higher self of the person you are testing. Check yourself first for any needed essences as a result of opening the coning.* Take your solution one time only. Then test the other person for needed essences as a result of opening the coning and administer the essences to him. These are also needed just one time. The steps for doing a Surrogate Basic Essence Test are listed on pages 71 to 74. (Non-Perelandra essences may be included for this Step.)

Step 2: Write the person's issue/problem and his symptoms. Urge him to give you all the symptoms he is experiencing whether he thinks they are part of the problem or not.

Step 3: You read aloud the intent. Remember that you are linking the focus and intent for the microbes connected with the person you are testing and not for your microbes.

Step 4: If this person's microbes don't need balancing for the issue in question, close the coning (remembering to disconnect both your higher

NOTE: For the sake of easier reading, I have written the surrogate testing information from the perspective of the reader testing a man. If you are testing a woman, mentally change all the pronouns to the appropriate feminine form. I am not making a political statement for having chosen to write this in the masculine. I tossed a coin to see which way I would go, and tails came up.

Temporarily disconnect physically from the person while you test yourself. Once you have taken any needed essences, physically make contact with the person again and repeat the above step 2. Then continue with the testing for Step 1.

self and the other person's higher self from the coning). If you know how to use the essences outside the Microbial Balancing Program, you may test the person for essences regarding this issue. You will be surrogate testing a regular essence test that does not need a coning. The regular surrogate essence testing steps are outlined in the guide that came with your Perelandra Essences. (To learn how to work with essences outside the Microbial Balancing Program, also see the book *Flower Essences*.)

If the issue tested positive for microbial balancing, go on to Step 5.

Step 5: Test which microbes in the person need testing and check the appropriate boxes. Then ask if they are to be tested as a unit or tested and treated separately. Whatever tests positive is how you are to proceed, and you will continue just as you would for yourself—only with your focus held on the person you are testing.

Step 6: Test the processes, checking the ones that test positive, and find out the order in which the processes are to be done.

The processes remain the same when surrogate testing another person. Remember that the processes are working with that person's microbes and body environment.

When you are testing essences, you will administer them to the other person—not to yourself. Once again, remember that they are for the *other person's* microbes or body environment as it relates to those microbes. If the person is interested and following what you are doing, you may have him hold the focus on why particular essences are being taken. Do this simply by telling him why the essences are needed and let him keep this in mind as you are putting the drops in his mouth and for about 10 seconds after. If he cannot do this, you hold that focus. The essences will automatically shift either way because of the connection between his electrical system and yours.

Test for essence dosage exactly as you would for yourself. If necessary, you may need to make a solution bottle for the person. To do the microbial balancing work properly, *you* will have to do any surrogate follow-up testing that is needed. (See p. 29.)

When shifting balancers from the spoon (and the few times you shift stabilizers from the spoon), just ask Pan to shift them appropriately to the other person. Modify what you normally would say when testing yourself to apply to working with the other person as you go through the Steps and processes in the Microbial Balancing Program. It's simply a matter of re-directing the focus from your microbes to the other person's microbes.

You may take short breaks (10 to 15 minutes) between the processes in Step 6 if needed, but don't take a break during a process, unless absolutely necessary.

Step 7: Use the Surrogate Basic Essence Test steps listed below. Keep in mind that the personal solution will be for the other person, not you.* You may need to make a solution bottle for these essences also. And you will have to do the surrogate follow-up testing when needed. (See p. 29.) You may include non-Perelandra essences for this Step.

(See p. 29.)

Make sure you (or the other person) focus on what these essences are for while they are being administered.

Step 8: Test for a troubleshooting recheck and a date.

Step 9: Close the coning, making sure you disconnect both your higher self and the person's higher self from the coning. Then test yourself for essences, including a dosage test.** This ensures that the work, the amount of focus that was required of you to do the work, the time you spent in the coning and the closing down of the coning have not adversely affected your balance. (Non-Perelandra essences may be included for this Step.)

*** Physically disconnect from the person while you test yourself. Once you have taken any needed essences, make physical contact with the person again and repeat step 2 of the Surrogate Testing Process setup. Then continue with the testing in Step 9.*

Once you have taken any needed essences one time, do a Surrogate Basic Essence Test for the other person to make sure nothing is needed for his balance as a result of the coning's impact on him. Use the steps listed below for the Surrogate Basic Essence Test.

Also, be aware of a possible protein drain for you and the other person. If one or both of you feels hungry or has a sudden craving for chocolate ice cream, that's an indication that a protein drain has occurred. Eat some nuts, then go for the ice cream.

Surrogate Basic Essence Test
for Steps 1, 7 and 9

1. Non-Perelandra essences may be included for Steps 1, 7 and 9 in the program. NOTE: When testing the other person in Steps 7 and 9, you will need to include a dosage test. Also, you will need to include a dosage test for yourself for Step 9.

2. If you have not already done this, physically make contact with the person you are going to test.*** Have him place a hand on your knee or

*** I have assumed you have already cleared yourself for surrogate testing the MBP and for any essences needed by you as a result of opening the coning.*

touch your foot with his foot. Focus on the person for a few seconds. This *touching and focusing* connects his electrical system to yours. Then test your connection using kinesiology asking (aloud or to yourself) if you are fully connected to this person's electrical system. If negative, spend a few more seconds focusing on the individual—and make sure you are physically touching. Then verify the connection again.

3. If the test for your connection to the other person was positive, you are ready to test for the essences. Place each box of bottles, one at a time, *in your lap* and ask:

"Does he need any of these essences from this box?" (Test.)

If you get a negative, you don't need to test the bottles from that box because none is needed.

If positive, place each bottle one at a time *in your lap* and ask if that essence is needed. A positive test response indicates that this particular essence rebalances the other person's system and makes it strong. (Remember, you have already cleared yourself of any need for the essences in the setup prior to starting the surrogate testing.) Double-check your results by placing the needed bottles *in the free hand or lap of the person*, and ask again if these are the essences needed.

If negative, make sure your connection with this person is still positive. Ask:

"Am I fully connected to this person's electrical system?"

If not, go back to step 2, relax, refocus on the person, and do the essence testing over again.

If you are connected, retest the other essences to find what was missed. Ask again:

"Are these all the essences needed?" (Test.)

If the response is positive, go on to step 4.*

* *If only one essence is needed, skip step 4 and go to step 5.*

If negative, you're still missing an essence. Keep retesting the other essences until you get a positive response to the question.

4. For a combination, place the combination bottles *in the person's free hand or lap*, and ask:

"Is this the combination he needs?" (Test.)

If negative, adjust the combination by removing any unnecessary essences. Test each separately by having the person hold it while you ask:

"Do I remove this bottle from the combination?" (Test.)

Whatever tests positive gets removed. Check the new combination by asking:

"Is this combination now correct?" (Test.)

Continue working with the combination until it tests positive.

5. Administer the essences needed either directly on the tongue or in a glass of water (add 9 drops of each needed essence concentrate to 4 ounces of water).* Have the person drink one good sip from this solution now and each time a dosage is administered. Make sure you (or the other person) focus on why these essences are being taken.

To preserve, add 3 teaspoons of brandy or distilled white vinegar. Refrigerate if no preservative is used.

6. An important component of the effectiveness of all essences is understanding. Therefore make sure that the person you are working with knows what essences are needed and how they are each defined.

Surrogate Testing for Dosage

Test for how many days/weeks and how many times a day the essences are needed. It is important that you remain physically connected with the other person throughout the testing process.

1. Place all the bottles that tested positive as a unit in the person's hands or lap.

2. Ask if he needs the essence(s) more than one time. If negative, that means he has already completed the dosage in step 5 of the Surrogate Basic Essence Test.

3. If positive, find out how many days he should take them and how many times per day. Do a sequential test. With the needed essence(s) in his lap, ask:

"Does he need these one day?" (Test.)

"2 days?" (Test.)

"3 days?" (Test.)

Do a count until you get a negative response. If the person needs to take the essences for 3 days, he will test positive when you ask, "1 day?", "2 days?", "3 days?" When you ask, "4 days?" he will test negative. That will tell you that the essences are needed for 3 days, not 4 days.

Daily Dosage

Using the same format, ask if he should take them:

"1 time daily?" (Test.)

"2 times daily?" (Test.)

And so on, until you get a negative. Your last positive will tell you how many times per day they are needed. Record the dosage on the chart.

If you wish to make a solution bottle, add *5 drops* of each essence needed to a half-ounce bottle. Then add a teaspoon of brandy or distilled white vinegar if you need to preserve the solution, and fill with spring or untreated water. If this is unavailable, tap water will do. You can also re-frigerate the solution, thus eliminating the need for preserving it with brandy or vinegar. Administer one dropperful (about 10 drops) of a pre-mixed solution for each dosage. (For children's solutions, see p. 77.)

Generally, essence solutions are to be administered first thing in the morning and/or last thing in the evening and/or in the mid-afternoon. If you wish to be more precise, test to see if it is best to administer them in the morning, afternoon or evening, or any combination of the three.

Remember to do the follow-up testing for this person once the dosage for each solution is completed.* (See p. 29.)

* Also make sure you (or the other person) focus on why these essences are being taken every time a dosage is administered.

IMPORTANT: While moving through the testing, it is important that the person you are testing be relaxed, yet quietly focused on the program. He can't read a book, listen to music, watch television, be continually dis-tracted by children or be allowed to fall into daydreaming. His attention to what is happening allows for accurate testing. If his mind is engaged in something else, your testing will be more difficult and possibly inaccurate. The easiest way to keep his attention is to say out loud what you are doing. When you can, explain what you are doing or which processes you are working with. Listening to you will keep him focused. If either of you is distracted, make sure *both of you* bring your attention back to the matter at hand before you continue with the testing.

SURROGATE TESTING CHILDREN

The Microbial Balancing Program is a critical tool to incorporate in the family's health regimen, especially with children. Kids are always "coming down with something." One of your first responses would be to check them for microbial balancing. And one of the best ways to break the pattern of your children always coming down with something is to test them monthly for microbial balancing needs. Also, if your children have ever been given an antibiotic, it is important to check them to see if their microbial balance was naturally restored after the antibiotic was used or if they have been left vulnerable by an imbalance. A constant flare-up of colds and other little infections may very well be the result of having taken antibiotics. I am not suggesting that antibiotics not be used in children's health. I am saying that even when they are used *properly*, they may leave a child's overall state of health out of balance as far as microbes are concerned and, therefore, vulnerable to recurring problems. You can break this cycle by using the Microbial Balancing Program. And, by testing children as soon as a problem becomes evident, you can help them work through many of the problems naturally without having to resort to antibiotics.

In general, you will be testing a child using the same method as for regular surrogate testing. But there are some issues that are unique to working with children under age twelve that you need to know about. I suggest that before working with a child, you first become familiar with the program by testing yourself until you feel comfortable with the Steps and processes. Then become comfortable doing the surrogate testing on some willing and needy adults. By becoming used to the program in this manner before working with children, you will be learning everything you need to know more gradually and it won't seem so overwhelming. In fact, if this whole chapter seems overwhelming, come back to it after you have worked with the program for yourself. It will seem quite manageable then.

Information Needed for Testing Children

INFANTS: Do not hold an infant while you are trying to work with the Microbial Balancing Program. First of all, your energy will impact and commingle with the child's energy field. This will alter the child's body environment and you won't be able to test her accurately. Also, you can't hold an infant, juggle all those bottles, do all that finger testing and write down the information. Something or someone is going to end up falling on to the floor.

ADMINISTERING STABILIZERS AND ESSENCES TO CHILDREN: My assumption is that your child is asleep for this testing because this is the

*NOTE: For the sake of fair play,
I have written the surrogate testing information in this section
from the perspective of the
reader testing a girl. If you are
testing a boy, mentally change
all the pronouns to the appropriate masculine form.*

* NOTE: *Children age twelve or older should be tested using the regular surrogate procedure. Mix any essence solutions the same as you would for adults. Anyone age twelve or over should be awake and cooperative with the testing.*

easiest way to test a small child. There are issues about doing all the balancing and stabilizing that is required in each of the processes and administering the stabilizer essences. The Microbial Balancing Program coning has accommodated these issues when testing children up to age twelve by giving a relatively simple solution.*

For the balancers, set up with Pan as you would in testing an adult, and ask that they be shifted from the spoon (that *you* will be holding) *to the child's microbes or area* in question.

Administer the stabilizers to children exactly as you would give them the balancers—have Pan shift them. Place one drop of each essence on a spoon and hold it out in front of you. Then set up with Pan and ask that the *stabilizers* be shifted appropriately to the child. Hold out the spoon for about 10 seconds, allowing for the shift, then wipe the spoon dry with a clean paper towel.

Use this process also when the child tests to take essences orally for the Essences Process in Step 6. NOTE: For children *up to age twelve,* you do not need to test for dosage for the Essences Process in Step 6. (There's some good news.) Assume that this solution will be needed *one time only* and it will be administered by Pan. Apply the solution as you would for an adult if the essences are to be soaking or topical—but again, it will be needed *one time only.* From age twelve on, you must test for dosage for the Essences Process in Step 6 and have the child take the solution as if she were an adult.

NOTE: This special Pan process for administering essences *does not apply to anyone age twelve or over who is not mentally or emotionally incapacitated.* It is assumed that "average" children twelve or older will be awake and consciously cooperating with the testing being done and not in need of special help. Also, microbes relate differently in a child's body environment than in an adult's. By age twelve, that relationship is considered "adult-like" and the one-time Pan application is not effective. If someone twelve or over is not cooperating with you, then you must consider if it is appropriate to be functioning as a surrogate tester for the Microbial Balancing Program with this person. You may be placing yourself in an "unethical" position in which you are bypassing an older child's conscious ability to participate in her own health regimen, even if you are the child's parent and have only the best intentions. In short, you may be manipulating this person. However, for those who are twelve or older, but who have special needs, such as mental retardation, severe hyperactivity or Attention Deficit Disorder (ADD), that make it *impossible* for them to participate in the testing, see the section in this chapter titled "Surrogate Testing Adults and Children with Special Needs."

HOLDING A SOLUTION FOCUS: Holding a focus while any multiple-day essence dosages are being administered alerts the child's body as to what is happening and why, and this, in turn, sets up the body appropriately for shifting the solution into the areas that correspond with the focus. In short, focus is a coordinating tool in the body. In case you are not sure what I mean by focus, all you need to do to accomplish the act is think about the purpose for the solution or state the purpose aloud to yourself or to the child directly.

For a young child, *you* will hold that focus while the child is taking the essences if she is not capable of or interested in thinking about the reason for the solution.* For an older child who you trust to take the solutions as prescribed, all you have to do is fix a solution bottle for each solution needed, label what each bottle is for and instruct the child to read the label every time the solution is taken.

* *Your focus impacts and influences the young child's electrical system, thus setting up the child's body for directing the essences into the appropriate areas.*

THE THREE PERSONAL SOLUTIONS FOR CHILDREN UNDER AGE TWELVE: There are 3 Steps on the chart where essences are tested for the person directly and not for that person's microbes: (1) in Step 1 after opening the coning, (2) in Step 7 for the personal solution, and (3) in Step 9 after closing the coning. For Step 1, you will administer any needed essences to the child by setting up the shift with Pan. However, it is important that the personal solutions for Steps 7 and 9 be given to the child directly. You have a couple of choices as to the best way to administer these essences for the Microbial Balancing Program.

1. If the child is *under nine months of age*, she can receive essences on her forehead. Her nervous system is still quite sensitive and can easily receive essences through the skin on the forehead area. Just place one drop of each needed essence on the forehead and gently rub the solution in with your finger.

2. The easiest way to do the microbial balancing testing for crawlers, toddlers and young children who will not sit still for you to put them through this routine is to do the testing while they are asleep. Give them

the personal Step 1 solution and the Step 6 balancers and stabilizers with Pan's help.

You will need to set up with Pan to shift the personal solutions for Steps 7 and 9 from the spoon to the sleeping child while you are doing the program. Then, *within the next 24 hours*, make sure the child *also* takes these solutions orally.* Give one essence solution at a time. Don't mix them into one super solution. For each, add *one drop* of each needed essence to *4 ounces* of water. The child does not have to drink the entire 4 ounces to receive the proper dosage. In fact, only 3 gulps are needed. By mixing the drops in 4 ounces of water, you will be diluting them to the point where she won't taste the brandy or vinegar that is used to preserve the essence concentrates.

* If you miss the 24-hour dead-line, administer the solution orally to the child as soon as you realize your mistake. Then open a coning for surrogate test-ing (including the child's higher self in the coning), and test the solution dosage (days/weeks/times per day) to see if there are any changes. You may need to extend the dosage an extra day or so because of the missed deadline.

Don't forget to state out loud or to yourself when you give the child the diluted solutions what each are for. (I'm repeating this several times because it is the easiest thing to forget, yet it is so important for administer-ing the essences correctly.) One will be the personal solution needed as a result of the microbial work and the other will be the solution needed for balancing after the coning is closed.

Children's essence dosages tend to be less complicated than the ones adults test for. Where an adult may need a personal solution of 8 essences for a week, 3 times a day, a child will tend to need just 2 essences for a couple of days, one time a day. Each time the child needs to take a dosage of the personal solutions they are to take directly (Steps 7 and 9), mix it in 4 ounces of water and hand it to her for the necessary 3 gulps while focus-ing on or saying what it is for. Or premix 4 ounces of diluted solution and dole it out *3 gulps at a time*, keeping the remaining solution in the refrig-erator for the next dosage. You cannot overdose a child with this solution. So if you'd like to mix the 4 ounces in a bottle and let the child drink from it for a couple of hours, this is fine. More than 3 gulps won't be an issue. However, less than 3 is an issue. (See p. 29.)

One last thing: Don't forget to do the follow-up testing for the child once the dosage for each solution is completed.

A NOTE ABOUT ESSENCES FOR CHILDREN: If you have found when testing Step 4 that your child's microbes do not need to be balanced as far as the stated focus in Step 2 is concerned, close the coning and test the child directly for this issue with essences. You will be surrogate testing a regular essence test that does not need a coning. It's a simple, regular, "normal" essence test. You already have the essences and you know how to kinesiology test, so you might as well learn how to use essences on a day-to-day basis. They are incredibly effective for many issues. And they are especially effective with children. The regular surrogate essence testing steps are outlined in the guide that came with your Perelandra Essences. (To learn more about how to work with essences with children outside the MBP, see the book *Flower Essences*.) Also, you can test for what the child needs using the Organizing Process chart. (See Appendix E.)

SURROGATE TESTING ADULTS
AND CHILDREN WITH SPECIAL NEEDS

By "special needs," I mean those individuals who are unconscious, semi-conscious, mentally and emotionally retarded and who have conditions such as severe hyperactivity or Attention Deficit Disorder (ADD). This does not include people who are capable of participating in the testing of the program with a little help on your part.

NOTE: *From here to the end of this chapter I have used the masculine pronouns.*

It is not ethical to open the coning and do the Microbial Balancing Program for someone eighteen years of age or over without his permission—and this includes someone with special needs. It is also not ethical to do the Microbial Balancing Program for anyone under age eighteen without the conscious permission of the child's parent(s) or guardian. If the person in need is capable of understanding a short description of the MBP work and answering for himself, describe the program simply and ask him if he'd like you to test him. Then do the regular Surrogate Testing Process as outlined for adults or children—whatever is appropriate. It is important that you be physically present with the person when you obtain the permission, do the testing, administer any "post-program" essence dosages, and do needed rechecks and follow-up. To test the program for someone who is incapable of understanding or answering, he may be asleep if this is the only way you will be able to get through the testing. To obtain permission from this person and to test the program for him, do the following:

1. Make physical contact with the person. For example, you can rest his hand on your arm or leg.

2. Ask to be connected to his higher self. Do this simply by saying:

"I'd like to be connected to _____'s higher self."
This will occur in about 10 seconds. Test using kinesiology to verify you are connected. If you test negative, you need to refocus, then request again to be connected. Verify the connection. This time you'll get a positive.

3. Quickly and simply explain the Microbial Balancing Program just as you would normally, and, in a simple yes/no format, ask if it is appropriate for you to open a Microbial Balancing Program coning and do the microbial balancing testing for him. (Test using kinesiology.)

This will work because you are now connected electrically with the person, and although he can't speak to you, he (his higher self) can still hear you and respond to what you are saying. You'll read his response electrically through the use of kinesiology.

4. If you get a positive response, open the MBP coning and do the surrogate testing as outlined for children under age twelve in this chapter. This will enable you to shift the balancers, stabilizers and essences to the person if or when he is unable to take them on his own.

5. You must administer any essence dosages that need to be taken once the coning is closed and do any of the follow-up testing. If the person cannot physically take an essence dosage (for example, he is unconscious), place a few drops of the pre-mixed solution on his lips. It will mix with his saliva and seep into his mouth.*

* Place 2 to 3 drops on the person's lips. Allow a little time for the drops to seep into his mouth and mix with his saliva. Then place another 2 to 3 drops on his lips. Keep doing this until a total of 10 drops has been administered. This procedure is effective, but it takes a little patience on your part. Make sure your intent is to be gentle, not invasive.

SURROGATE TESTING THE MICROBIAL BALANCING PROGRAM FOR PROFESSIONALS

I feel strongly that a person who wishes to offer the Microbial Balancing Program to others must be familiar and comfortable with the program first—and this especially includes professionals who wish to add the program to their health practice. If you already use kinesiology in your practice, I recommend that you frequently work with the program personally for at least 6 months before offering it to others. If you must learn kinesiology along with the program, I recommend that you work with both for a year frequently before offering it in your practice.

To become familiar with surrogate testing before "going public," there's always members of your family and friends who are in need of microbial balancing. Working with them will also give you a chance to practice explaining the Microbial Balancing Program and the coning to others. It can be done—honest. And you can do it without embarrassing yourself. You just need to take a little time to think about how to describe this concept to others using language that is comfortable to you and them. One professional in Ireland who uses several Perelandra processes in her practice and who has tackled the communication problem wrote:

It may be useful to others to hear how I ask clients in this conservative area if I can connect to their higher selves. After I've done my normal diagnostic work involving lots of questions and a physical exam, I tell the client that my intent in all my work is to work in harmony with that highest part of themselves, however they conceive of it—their spirit, their soul, their higher selves. I say that I feel I can do this most effectively if I inwardly ask to consciously connect with them at that level whenever they are here for a treatment. I ask them if that is alright. When I use this approach, there is unanimous consent—usually with genuine appreciation. I then inwardly do the connecting and disconnecting at each session.

There are a few clients who I do inform of my work with nature and MAP. Mostly, however, I don't. I think that over time there will be more and more clients I can share with more openly. . . .

With some clients it may be appropriate (and easier) to loan them a copy of this book and suggest that they read the Introduction and Chapter 1.

Once you become familiar with the program personally and as a surrogate tester, it is easy to incorporate the program into your practice. To do this, you must have the following:

- *conscious* permission from your client for you to open the coning and work with the Microbial Balancing Program,

- the five sets of the Perelandra Essences,

- the Perelandra Expanded Balancing Process Kit,

- a tablespoon, paper towels, a watch or clock and a calendar, and

- any non-Perelandra flower essences you wish to include in your client's personal testing for Steps 1, 7 and 9.

OTHER POINTS TO FOLLOW: You must set up and use the coning only as indicated in the program. You cannot "customize" the coning to your own liking if you want it to be effective.

You must be willing to facilitate the process by surrogate testing your client. This means that the time needed to move someone through the program must be allowed for in the appointment. You won't be able to run in and out of the room attending to other clients while the coning is open and the person is moving through the program Steps.

SCHEDULING SUGGESTION: You may integrate this program into your practice without creating chaos with your schedule just as you can integrate it into your personal life. The problem, of course, is that when testing someone for microbial balancing you won't know ahead of time how many processes they will need or how long it will take you to move the person through the testing. I make the same suggestion to you as I have made to individuals facing a time problem:

1. Set up and test program Steps 1 through 5 for the person during the initial office visit. For Step 6 (Troubleshooting List), test what processes you need to surrogate. Do not find out what order they are to be done in.

2. Estimate the time you will need for surrogating the processes that tested positive and schedule the person for that amount of time *within the next 48 hours.*

3. At the second appointment, open the coning, test for essences for both of you and read aloud Steps 2, 3 and 5. This reestablishes the focus and intent for the work. You will not need to retest Step 6 for what processes are needed. However, you now need to find out what order you are to do them in. Once you have this information, proceed with the process testing and, when Step 6 is completed, continue through the remaining Steps.

NOTE: If your hectic practice makes it impossible for you to schedule a block of time within 48 hours after this initial testing, you'll still have an idea about how extensive the work will be from the above steps 1 and 2. Estimate the block of time you will need based on this information, then schedule the person for when that time is available. If the second appointment is scheduled beyond the 48-hour time limit, start the program testing from the beginning and use a new chart. You may test for the same processes in Step 6 as you did the first time or there may be a small change. Either way, you'll be able to do the needed testing within the block of time you have allotted.

While moving through the testing, it is important that your client be relaxed, yet quietly focused on the program. He can't read a book, listen to music on a Walkman or be allowed to fall into daydreaming. His attention to what is happening allows for accurate testing. If his mind is engaged in something else, your testing will be more difficult and possibly inaccurate. The easiest way to keep his attention is to say out loud what you are doing. When you can, explain what you are doing or which processes you are working with. Listening to you will keep him focused. If either of you is distracted, make sure *both of you* bring your attention back to the matter at hand before you continue with the testing.

You must be sure that the client has a solution bottle for any needed essence dosages that extend beyond the office visit. Be sure to label the bottles well, including how many days the person is to take the solution, how many times a day and what the solution is for. Then you will need to instruct the client on how to administer the dosage and to focus on what each solution is for as they are taking the dose.

You must take responsibility for surrogating all the client's follow-ups and rechecks.

Working in a coning for long periods of time may cause a protein drain. Be aware of how you feel, and increase your protein intake on the days you are scheduled to surrogate the Microbial Balancing Program. Also, it would be good to have protein—like nuts—available for your clients in case they also experience such a drain. If they come out of the coning saying they crave sweets, this is a good sign they are experiencing a protein drain.

AN IMPORTANT POINT ABOUT THE CONING: Even though you may not physically see the members of this coning (other than yourself and your client), it does not mean that they can be manipulated. If you do not obtain *conscious* permission to use the program and the coning from your client, the members of the coning will not allow you to place them in a position of manipulating this person. They'll know as soon as you open the coning that you are trying to sneak something over on someone—even though your intentions may only be the best for this person. Under these circumstances, they will not engage in the testing process and will simply wait in a holding pattern until you close the coning. The testing you do as you try to move through the Steps will be inaccurate because the information is not coming from the coning. It is coming from you. Also, the coning members will not engage in the testing process if you try to customize the coning.

Chapter 5

Using the Microbial Balancing Program for Land, Sea, Air and Animals

The same principles that apply to microbial balancing for the human body also apply equally to microbial balancing in other environmental situations. Microbes are everywhere. It is important to all environments that their microbes be addressed when needed. It is also important to the quality of our health that microbial balance within the environments in which we live and work be maintained. Farmers, gardeners and people who work to maintain environmental health in land, forests, ponds and lakes will want to utilize the Microbial Balancing Program. As with the human body, you can do a monthly general balancing for microbes within any other defined environment, and you can also do microbial balancing around specific issues or problems. In Chapter 1, I mentioned that I have been working with microbial balancing in the Perelandra garden for years. It is an essential part of the garden's maintenance, and it is this focus that is the foundation for the Microbial Balancing Program.

Before you faint at the notion of broadening the use of the program beyond the human body, let me say that applying it to these new areas is a

*All environmental essence
stabilizers and solutions, as
well as the balancers, will be
shifted from a spoon. Do not
take them orally.*

snap. You only have to make a couple of changes. First, you'll need to adjust the coning a bit to take into account the different host environments. (See the list of environmental conings in this chapter.) And second, you will function as the surrogate tester and use the Surrogate Essence Testing as written, except for one change: When testing environments, *all* balancers, stabilizers and essence solutions will be shifted from a spoon with Pan's help as set up in the Balancing and Stabilizing Process in Chapter 3.* The "person" you are surrogate testing is the land, sea, air or animal. You do not have to maintain physical contact with these host environments during the testing, but it might be easier to maintain your focus if you are present at the site or in the same room with the animal.

The rest of the program applies to the microbes in these different situations as it applies to humans because, as far as nature is concerned, a microbe is a microbe is a microbe—no matter what its environment.

NOTE: Before working with the processes in this chapter, it is important that you first do the Microbial Balancing Program for yourself and become comfortable working with the chart. This will acquaint you with the program and prepare you for doing microbial balancing for land, sea, air and animals. I have written this chapter assuming that there are many things that I explained in the earlier chapters that I do not have to repeat here. Also, I recommend that you read this chapter thoroughly several times before using the Microbial Balancing Program with environments or animals.

A SUGGESTION: Record the members of the coning you are working with on the back of the chart. You will need to open this coning when administering essence dosages, and it will be easier to read the list of coning members from the chart than to look it up each time in this manual.

To figure out how much time to allot for the testing of the program, you may use the same scheduling approach with environmental and animal testing as is used with human testing.

1. Set up and test program Steps 1 through 5. For Step 6 (Troubleshooting List), test what processes you need to surrogate. Do not find out what order they are to be done in.

2. Estimate the time you will need for surrogating the processes that tested positive and schedule that amount of time *within the next 48 hours*.

3. The second session: Open the appropriate coning, test yourself for

essences and read Steps 2, 3 and 5. This reestablishes the focus and intent for the work. You will not need to retest Step 6 for what processes are needed. However, you now need to find out what order you are to do them in. Once you have this information, proceed with the process testing and, when Step 6 is completed, continue through the remaining Steps.* Don't forget you may take short breaks between the processes in Step 6, if needed. However, unless absolutely necessary—such as needing to go to the bathroom—do not take breaks during the processes. Also remember that you may take short breaks, if needed, between the Steps.

AN IMPORTANT NOTE ABOUT DOING MICROBIAL BALANCING FOR DIFFERENT ENVIRONMENTS: It is not appropriate to do the Microbial Balancing Program on land that you do not own or are not renting. In an office building, it is only appropriate to do the program for your office or work space, not the entire building. It is never appropriate to decide for others what is best for them, even if you think the Microbial Balancing Program is the most beneficial thing around. Focus only on the environments for which you are directly responsible and don't impose yourself or this program on others without their conscious permission.

* If you miss the 48-hour deadline, you will need to start the testing over and use a new chart.

SURROGATE TESTING PROCESS
FOR LAND, SEA AND AIR

1. SETUP: Always clear yourself just before testing an environment. State aloud or to yourself: "I would like to prepare myself for surrogate testing the Microbial Balancing Program." Then do the basic essence test for yourself and take any needed essences. You do not need to test for dosage. These essences will be taken one time only.

NOTE: Non-Perelandra essences may be used when the testing applies to you, the surrogate tester, directly (Steps 1 and 9). *However, when essence testing for an environment and its microbes, you will need to use only the five sets of Perelandra Essences.*

2. Spend a moment either looking directly at or picturing in your mind the area you wish to work with. This focuses you on the environment.

3. You are ready to test the MBP. Using a new chart, write a short description of the issue being tested and the date on the first line.

NOTE: Insects maintain their microbial balance as a direct result of the microbial work that is done for land, sea and air. Consequently, insects do not need a microbial balancing process designed especially for them. Also, insects alert us when there is an environmental problem. If you observe an imbalance among the insect population around you, take this as a sign that there is an environmental problem that needs addressing. Test the Microbial Balancing Program and the environmental processes in both Workbooks to determine what is needed.

Surrogate Testing the Chart

Step 1: Open the appropriate coning as described in this chapter for the specific environment you are working with. Check yourself for any needed essences as a result of opening the coning. Take your solution one time only. (You do not need to test the environment.)

Step 2: Describe the problem/issue that you wish to address.

Step 3: Read the intent. Remember that you are linking the focus and intent for the microbes in the environment you are testing and not for your microbes.

Step 4: If this environment's microbes don't need balancing for the issue in question, close the coning (Step 9) and test the troubleshooting chart in Chapter 11 in *Workbook II* regarding this issue.

If the issue tested positive for microbial balancing, go on to Step 5.

Step 5: Test which microbes in the environment need balancing and check the appropriate boxes. Then ask if they are to be tested as a unit or tested and treated separately. Whatever tests positive is how you are to proceed, and you will continue just as you would have for yourself—only with your focus maintained on this environment and its microbes.

Step 6: Test the Troubleshooting List, checking the processes that test positive, and find out the order in which the processes are to be done.

The processes remain the same when surrogate testing an environment. Remember that the processes are working with that environment as the host and *its* microbes. In the processes, modify any wording of the statements you are to make to reflect that you are now working with an environment and its microbes and not a human and his/her microbes. For example, in the Energy Cleansing Process as written in Chapter 3, you state in step 4, "I ask that any inappropriate, stagnant, darkened or ungrounded energies be released from *my body environment*." When stating this for an environmental microbial balancing, you will state, "I ask that any inappropriate, stagnant, darkened or ungrounded energies be released from *this environment*."

When you are testing the Essences Process, you will administer the essences to the environment with the help of Pan.* Test for an essence dosage as you would for yourself. If necessary, make a solution bottle. And, to

* Use the Basic Essence Test for Microbes and Their Environment when testing.

Also, you do not need to test the boxes for how the essences are to be administered. They will be shifted with Pan's help—a nature spirit application.

do the microbial balancing work properly, you will have to do any surrogate follow-up testing that is needed for the Essences Process. *Each time a dosage is to be administered, open the appropriate environmental Microbial Balancing Program coning and set up with Pan for shifting the dosage to the microbes and/or their environment.*

* During the shift, make sure you focus on what these essences are for.

When shifting balancers *and* stabilizers from the spoon in the processes in Step 6, just ask Pan to shift them appropriately to the environment or its microbes (or both)—whatever the focus. Again, modify what you normally would say to apply to working with the microbes and/or their environment.

Step 7: The personal solution will be *for the environment.* Use the Surrogate Basic Essence Test for Environments steps. You may wish to make a solution bottle for these essences also, if a multiple-day dosage is needed. And you will have to do the surrogate follow-up testing when needed. Each time a dosage is to be administered, open the appropriate environmental MBP coning and set up with Pan for shifting about 10 drops of the solution dosage from the spoon to the environment.*

Step 8: Test for a troubleshooting recheck and a date.

Step 9: Close the coning. Then test *yourself* for essences and *include a dosage test.*** This ensures that the work, the amount of focus that was required of you to do the work, the time you spent in the coning and the closing down of the coning have not adversely impacted your balance. (Non-Perelandra essences may be included for this Step.) You do not need to test the environment for further essence balancing.

** Use the Basic Essence Test for Humans.

Be aware of a possible protein drain for you.

Surrogate Basic Essence Test for Environments for Step 7

1. I assume that you have cleared yourself as the surrogate tester with essences, the appropriate Microbial Balancing Program coning is already open and you have tested yourself again for essences needed because of the coning impact. If not, do so now. (Non-Perelandra essences may be included when testing yourself.)

2. You are ready to test for the essences for the environment. Place the sets one box at a time in your lap and ask:

"Does the environment need any of these essences?" (Test.)

If you get a negative, you don't need to test the bottles from that box because none is needed.

If positive, place each bottle one at a time in your lap and ask if that essence is needed. A positive test response indicates that this particular essence rebalances the environment in light of the microbial balancing work that has been done. Check your results by placing all the needed bottles in your lap and asking again if these are the essences needed.

If negative, retest the other essences to find what was missed. Ask again:

"Are these all the essences needed?" (Test.)

If the response is positive, go on to step 3.*

If negative, you're still missing an essence. Keep retesting the other essences until you get a positive response to the question.

3. For a combination, place the combination bottles in your lap, and ask:

"Is this the combination this environment needs?" (Test.)

If negative, adjust the combination by removing any unnecessary essences. Test each bottle separately, asking:

"Do I remove this bottle from the combination?" (Test.)

Whatever tests positive gets removed. Check the new combination by asking:

"Is this combination now correct?" (Test.)

Continue working on the combination until it tests positive.

4. Administer the essences needed with the help of Pan.** After testing for dosage (see below), you may wish to prepare a solution bottle. Don't forget to focus on what the solution is for while it is being shifted.

Testing for Dosage

Test for how many days/weeks and how many times a day you are to administer the essences using the same yes/no testing procedure you used on yourself. Environmental essence balancing tends to be less complex than what is required for humans, so don't expect lengthy dosages.***

1. Place in your lap all the bottles that tested positive as a unit.

2. Ask if you need to make this combination available to the environment more than one time. If negative, that means the dosage is already completed in the above step 4.

Footnotes:

* If only one essence is needed, skip step 3 and go to step 4.

** Put one drop of each needed essence into the spoon.

*** However, where there is serious imbalance, these dosages may be more on the complex side.

3. If positive, find out how many days you should make these essences available to the environment and how many times per day. Do a sequential test. With the needed essences in the your lap, ask:

"Are these essences needed one day?" (Test.)

"2 days?" (Test.)

"3 days?" (Test.)

"4 days?" (Test.)

Do a count until you get a negative response. If the essences are needed for 3 days, it will test positive when you ask, "1 day?", "2 days?", "3 days?" When you ask "4 days?" it will test negative. That will tell you that the essences are needed for 3 days, not 4 days.

Daily Dosage

Using the same format, ask if the essences should be made available:

"1 time daily?" (Test.)

"2 times daily?" (Test.)

"3 times daily?" (Test.)

And so on, until you get a negative. Your last positive will tell you how many times per day they are needed. Record the dosage on the chart.

If you need to make a solution bottle, add *3 drops* of each essence needed to a half-ounce bottle. Then add a teaspoon of brandy or distilled white vinegar if you need to preserve the solution, and fill with spring or untreated water. If this is unavailable, tap water will do. When shifting this solution with Pan, put one dropperful of the solution (about 10 drops) into the spoon for the shift.

As with humans, essences for environments are to be administered in the morning and/or in the evening and/or in the mid-afternoon. If you wish to be more precise, test to see if it is best to administer them in the morning, afternoon or evening, or any combination of the three. Again, don't expect a complex daily dosage for environments. *And remember that you will be opening the coning for the environment you are working with each time you administer a dosage.* You will also need to focus on what the solution is for every time a dosage is being shifted.

Don't forget to do the follow-up testing once the dosage for each solution is completed. (See p. 29.)

LAND, SOIL, PLANT AND WATER CONINGS

Coning for Land Areas

The coning for land areas includes:

1. The devas of the Microbial Balancing Program, Viruses, Fungi, Bacteria, Protozoa, *PLUS* the deva of the land area you wish to do a microbial balancing with: garden, back yard, a specific field, a farm, woods, entire property that you own . . . Include the deva of whatever the host environment is that you are focusing the work on. (Examples: Ask to be connected to the "deva of my garden," "deva of the north field" or "deva of our property.")

2. Pan

3. The appropriate connection with the White Brotherhood for the Microbial Balancing Program for environments

4. Your higher self

Wait 10 seconds or verify the connection for each member of the coning as you state its name aloud, then (so you may adjust to the coning) wait another 10 to 15 seconds after every member is connected. Test yourself for essences and proceed with the Surrogate Testing Process.*

* *Use the Surrogate Testing Process for Land, Sea and Air beginning on p. 87.)*

Coning for Soil

Checking for microbial balancing is especially helpful for gardens, greenhouses, compost piles, backyards, farms and forests.

The coning for soil includes:

1. The devas of the Microbial Balancing Program, Viruses, Fungi, Bacteria, Protozoa, *PLUS* the deva of the land area that you are focusing the work on *and* the Deva of Soil

2. Pan

3. The appropriate connection with the White Brotherhood for the Microbial Balancing Program for environments

4. Your higher self

Wait 10 seconds or verify the connection for each member of the coning as you state its name aloud, then (so you may adjust to the coning) wait another 10 to 15 seconds after every member is connected. Test essences for yourself and proceed with the Surrogate Testing Process.

Coning for Plants

For plants, you will need to address two separate but related issues: (1) the plant itself, and (2) the soil and its microbes surrounding the plant.* You will need two charts. If you have a plant with a disease, you will test the plant (or plants of the same variety with the same problem) on one chart and its soil on the other chart. If more than one plant variety appears to be having the same problem, you will have to test the varieties separately, using a new chart and an appropriately adjusted coning for each variety. You will use a new chart for testing the soil for each variety. Use the coning below for the plant and use the coning for soil for its soil.**

The coning for plants includes:

1. The devas of the Microbial Balancing Program, Viruses, Fungi, Bacteria, Protozoa, *PLUS* the deva of the specific plant*** (or multiple plants of the *same* variety in a garden, field or forest) that you wish to focus the work on

2. Pan

3. The appropriate connection with the White Brotherhood for the Microbial Balancing Program for environments

4. Your higher self

Wait 10 seconds or verify the connection for each member of the coning as you state its name aloud, then (so you may adjust to the coning) wait another 10 to 15 seconds after every member is connected. Test essences for yourself and proceed with the Surrogate Testing Process.

BODIES OF WATER

Although I used the word "sea" in the title of this chapter, consider that writer's license. Unless you own a sea or are responsible for its maintenance, it won't be appropriate for you to do microbial balancing for one. However, if your land contains a lake or pond, or if you own or are responsible for a portion of a lake or pond, you can use the program. In the second situation, you will be addressing the balance only for the portion of the lake or pond for which you are responsible. If you wish to work with a stream, you will be focusing on the portion of the stream that runs through your land. Because the water is constantly flowing through, this may seem like a useless exercise. But the MBP will improve your portion of the

* *The volume of soil that is worked with varies among plants. When testing a plant's soil, simply state to the coning that you wish to focus the work on this plant's soil. The coning will automatically define what constitutes that plant's soil, and the program testing will be in light of this definition.*

** *When testing potted plants, you will test the plant itself, then test the soil in the container by opening the coning for soil. In this case, the land area is defined by the soil environment contained in the pot.*

*** *Examples: the Deva of Broccoli, the Deva of Crookneck Yellow Squash, the Deva of Nasturtium . . . If you don't know the name of the plant, point to it or touch it and ask that the deva of this plant be included in the MBP coning for plants.*

stream. And, the downstream portion will benefit from the microbial balancing you achieve on the portion that runs through your land. The same principle holds true for working with "a piece" of a pond or lake. The "pieces" surrounding yours will benefit from the balance achieved in your "piece."

NOTE: A body of water is a complex environment. To achieve microbial balance, you may need to address the soil surrounding and containing that body. For this you will need two charts. One for the body of water (which includes all plant life within the water and on its surface) and the other chart for the soil surrounding and containing the water. Add the Deva of Soil to the coning for bodies of water for this soil testing. If you are addressing a specific problem with plant life in the water, still approach the testing with these two focuses—the body of water and its surrounding soil. The plants are considered part of the body of water and, to achieve microbial balance in these plants, the microbes for the entire body of water must be addressed.

However, if you have potted plants in a plastic- or cement-lined pond, you will have to treat the plants independently and test the microbial balance for them (using the coning for plants) plus the soil in each plant's pot (add the Deva of Soil to the coning for bodies of water), as well as test the water and soil surrounding the pond. In this case, you start testing with four charts. If you are still testing that microbial balancing is needed for a problem, but the testing for the plants, pot soil, surrounding soil and water is negative, check the pond liner. Perhaps there is a microbial imbalance in or on the liner that is causing the problem. In this case you will be starting with five charts. Test each of the five charts through Step 4 to determine the problem areas that are in need of microbial balancing. More often than not, you will need to get into the processes in Step 6 on only one chart.* The other four charts will ensure that you have covered all your bases for the problem you wish to address. In short, if you don't cover these bases and you miss balancing all the microbes involved, you will not get the desired results from the program and you will have put out effort for naught.

THE GOOD NEWS: When doing *a general balancing* for a body of water, all the elements contained within that body—plants, algae, soil, rocks and water—are included in the balancing, and you start with only *one* chart!

* Work multiple charts as you would for human host environments. Test for the order they are to be worked.

Coning for Bodies of Water

The coning for bodies of water includes:

1. The devas of the Microbial Balancing Program, Viruses, Fungi, Bacteria, Protozoa, *PLUS* the deva of the pond, lake or stream area that you are focusing the work on (Examples: Define a stream area by asking to be connected to "the deva of the stream that runs through our property." Define your portion of a lake or pond by asking to be connected to "the deva of the portion of the lake/pond for which I am responsible.")

2. Pan

3. The appropriate connection with the White Brotherhood for the Microbial Balancing Program for environments

4. Your higher self

Wait 10 seconds or verify the connection for each member of the coning as you state its name aloud, then (so you may adjust to the coning) wait another 10 to 15 seconds after every member is connected. Test essences for yourself and proceed with the Surrogate Testing Process.

When addressing the microbes in the surrounding soil, add the Deva of Soil to the coning for bodies of water.

When addressing the microbes in potted water plants, use the coning for plants and add the Deva of Soil to the coning for bodies of water when checking the soil in the pots.

When addressing the microbes in or on a pond liner, add the deva of the liner of your pond to the coning for bodies of water.

When addressing specific problems with aquatic animal life, use the coning for mammals, fish, fowl and reptiles. But also make sure the problem isn't being caused by a microbial imbalance in the water, potted plants and their soil and surrounding soil.

ATMOSPHERE

If you have an environmental microbial situation that needs to be addressed, but the testing for land, plants, sea and soil are coming up negative, test the environmental balance in the atmosphere surrounding the site. In fact, make it a point to always determine if the atmosphere needs to be microbially balanced along with the land, plants, sea and soil. And if you simply wish to do general balancing as a preventive measure for your home and office environments, don't forget to include a general balancing for the atmosphere. *For this testing, you will focus on the one-half-mile tall "air dome" that permeates and surrounds the site in question. Instead of soil, you will be working with air.*

Coning for Atmosphere

The coning for atmosphere includes:

1. The devas of the Microbial Balancing Program, Viruses, Fungi, Bacteria, Protozoa, *PLUS* the Deva of Atmosphere

2. Pan

3. The appropriate connection with the White Brotherhood for the Microbial Balancing Program for environments

4. Your higher self

Wait 10 seconds or verify the connection for each member of the coning as you state its name aloud, then (so you may adjust to the coning), wait another 10 to 15 seconds after every member is connected. Test essences for yourself and proceed with the Surrogate Testing Process.

BUILDINGS, HOMES, APARTMENTS, OFFICES

You may use the Microbial Balancing Program to address problems and issues related to buildings or portions of buildings (such as single rooms and apartments). This would include mold, mildew and the various indoor pollution problems that we are often plagued with. In these situations, you will be able to work with only those buildings or portions of buildings for which you are responsible. The microbes inside an interior space interact with the host environment much the same as the microbes inside and around a human body.

NOTE: You can only balance microbes for the *true* environment in which they live. For example, if you live in a basement apartment that maintains the humidity level similar to the inside of a cave, the program will adjust the microbes' balance to this cavelike environment—even if you call it an apartment. In order to change the microbial activity in your apartment, you must first do something about the humidity level. In short, if you'd like the microbial activity to resemble that which is appropriate for an apartment, you will have to first supply an interior environment that resembles an apartment.

ADDITIONAL POINTS: If you are working with the microbial balance of an interior environment, you may not be able to address the situation fully if you focus solely on the *interior* of a building. You may need to include testing for the soil base upon which the building stands (use the coning for land) and the atmosphere that surrounds the building (use the coning for atmosphere). When addressing an interior situation, be sure to check these exterior conditions that may be adversely affecting the interior balance.

If you do not own or rent the whole building and the land upon which it sits (such as your office or apartment), you will have to confine your testing to the interior area that you are responsible for. You won't be able to do any work with the building's soil base. However, because of the unique, mutable nature of atmosphere and the fact that no one owns it, you may include working with the atmosphere surrounding the building.

Coning for Buildings and Indoor Environments

The coning for buildings and indoor environments includes:

1. The devas of the Microbial Balancing Program, Viruses, Fungi, Bacteria, Protozoa, *PLUS* the deva of the building, home, barn, apartment, office, etc.*

2. Pan

3. The appropriate connection with the White Brotherhood for the Microbial Balancing Program for environments

4. Your higher self

Wait 10 seconds or verify the connection for each member of the coning as you state its name aloud, then (so you may adjust to the coning) wait another 10 to 15 seconds after every member is connected. Test essences for yourself and proceed with the Surrogate Testing Process.

* Examples: Ask to be connected to "the deva of our home," "the deva of my apartment," "the deva of my office" or "the deva of the chicken coop next to the north field."

MAMMALS, FISH, FOWL, REPTILES

You will do the Microbial Balancing Program for mammals, fish, fowl and reptiles using the following Surrogate Testing Process for Animals and Surrogate Basic Essence Test for Animals. If you recognize the steps, it's because they are essentially the same testing processes used for land, soil, water and air—except for some modified wording and two changes.

1. FOR MAMMALS: The essences that are needed for the Essences Process in Step 6 and the solutions needed for Step 7 will be administered to the mammal orally. If the solution cannot be given orally while the coning is open, they must be shifted at that point by Pan. Then administer the solution orally to the mammal *within 24 hours* of the program testing.

All the balancers and stabilizers will be shifted from the spoon to the mammal with the help of Pan.

FOR FISH, FOWL AND REPTILES: *All* essence solutions, balancers and stabilizers will be shifted with the help of Pan. If in Steps 6 and 7 a multiple-day dosage is needed, you will need to open the Microbial Balancing Program coning for mammals, fish, fowl and reptiles each time and set up with Pan to assist you in shifting the solution.

2. You must open the same coning for all the multiple-day essence dosages given to mammals, fish, fowl and reptiles, whether the essences are administered directly (orally) or shifted by Pan. For example, if a dog needs an essence solution for 3 days, 2 times a day, the coning must be opened each time that solution is administered. You'll just open the coning, administer any solutions that are needed (focusing on what the solution is for), then close the coning again. You won't have to test yourself for essences since the coning will be open for such a short period of time.

Coning for Animals

The coning for animals (mammals, fish, fowl and reptiles) includes:

1. The devas of the Microbial Balancing Program, Viruses, Fungi, Bacteria, Protozoa, *PLUS* the Deva of Animal Healing (This deva holds the healing patterns for all mammals, fish, fowl and reptiles.)

2. Pan

3. The appropriate connection with the White Brotherhood for the Microbial Balancing Program *for animals*

4. Your higher self *and the animal's higher self* (State: "I'd like to be connected to this animal's higher self.")

Wait 10 seconds or verify the connection for each member of the coning as you state its name aloud, then (so you may adjust to the coning) wait another 10 to 15 seconds after every member is connected. Test essences for yourself, taking the needed essences one time only, and proceed with the Surrogate Testing Process for Animals listed below.*

Surrogate Testing Process for Animals

1. SETUP: Always clear yourself just before surrogate testing an animal. State aloud or to yourself: "I would like to prepare myself for surrogate testing the Microbial Balancing Program." Then do a basic test for yourself and take any needed essences. You do not need to test for dosage. These essences will be taken one time only.

* The animal does not need to be tested for this step.

NOTE: Non-Perelandra essences may be used when the testing applies to you, the surrogate tester, directly. *However, when essence testing for an animal and its microbes, you will need to use only the five sets of Perelandra Essences.*

2. Spend a moment either looking directly at or picturing in your mind the animal you wish to work with. This focuses your attention on the animal. You do not need to maintain direct physical contact with the animal during MBP testing.

3. You are ready to test the Microbial Balancing Program. Using a new chart, write the animal's name, a short description of the issue being tested and the date on the first line.

Surrogate Testing the Chart for Animals

Step 1: Open the coning for the animal you are working with. Check yourself for any needed essences as a result of opening the coning. Take your essences one time only. The animal does not need to be tested.

Step 2: Describe the problem/issue that you wish to address regarding this animal.

Step 3: Read the intent. Remember that you are linking the focus and intent for the *animal's* microbes and not for your microbes.

Step 4: If this animal's microbes don't need balancing for the issue in question, close the coning (Step 9) and work with the Nature Healing Coning for Animals. (See the book *MAP* and Perelandra Paper #8.**)

If the issue tested positive for microbial balancing, go on to Step 5.

** See the order form in the back of this manual.

Step 5: Test which microbes need balancing and check the appropriate boxes. Then ask if they are to be tested as a unit or tested and treated separately. Whatever tests positive is how you are to proceed, and you will continue just as you would have for yourself—only with your focus maintained on this animal's microbes and their host environment.

Step 6: Test the Troubleshooting List, checking the processes that test positive, and find out the order in which the processes are to be done.

The processes remain the same when surrogate testing an animal. (Remember that the processes are working with that animal as the host environment and its microbes.) In the processes, modify any wording of the statements you make to reflect that you are now working with an animal and its microbes and not a human and his/her microbes.

ESSENCE SOLUTION FOR MAMMALS: (For this section and the next, I use "animal" to refer to mammals only.) The essences that are needed for the Essences Process in Step 6 will be given orally to the animal.* If the animal is asleep at the time of testing, the first dosage of these solutions must be administered by Pan while the coning is open and while doing the processes. Make sure the animal drinks some of the solution *within 24 hours* of the program testing—even if they are to receive this solution just one time.** For this, you must open the coning for mammals, fish, fowl and reptiles. It is important that mammals receive the essences both during the program testing and at least one time directly. If you can give the dosage directly while doing the Essences Process, you eliminate the need to administer the essences that additional time. If the dosage is to be given for a couple of days, open the coning each time, hold the focus for why the solution is being given and administer each needed solution orally. You may be giving the animal two or more solutions, so be sure you focus on what each solution is for while the animal is drinking it. Also be sure to test for dosage and do any needed follow-up essence testing.

NOTE: All the balancers and stabilizers will be shifted from a spoon to mammals with the help of Pan.

ADMINISTERING ORAL SOLUTIONS TO MAMMALS: Sometimes animals will lick the drops right out of your hand. You may also squirt a dropperful of the pre-mixed, half-ounce solution into an animal's mouth using a plastic dropper. (Be sure to wash the dropper well after using it.) Or you can put those drops directly on food. However, if the animal is put off by the

* Do not test the boxes on the chart for how these essences are to be administered. They will be given orally or they will be shifted from a spoon with Pan's help (a nature spirit application). How they are to be given is already set up for you in the instructions and steps.

** If you miss the 24-hour deadline, open the coning and administer the solution orally as soon as you realize your mistake. Then, before closing the coning, test the solution dosage again to see if there are any changes. You may need to extend the dosage an extra day or so because of the missed deadline.

brandy smell or taste, you will need to be creative. To mask the brandy, you can dilute the solution by mixing *one drop of each needed essence in 2 ounces of water*. The animal only has to drink 3 teaspoons of this diluted mixture each time you administer a dose. You can pour the 3 teaspoons over the animal's food. If further bribing is needed, choose a treat they can't resist and spoon the solution over the treat. Then store the rest of the diluted solution in the refrigerator for the next dose. If all else fails, stick their front paw into a bowl of the diluted solution several times and let them lick it off. While they are licking, don't forget to focus on what the solution is addressing.

Be sure to do all needed essence follow-up testing (p. 29). And continue to open the coning each time you give these solutions to the animal.

FOR FISH, FOWL AND REPTILES: *All* essence solutions, balancers and stabilizers will be shifted from the spoon with the help of Pan. If in Steps 7 and 9 an essence dosage is needed for a couple of days, you will need to open the Microbial Balancing Program coning for mammals, fish, fowl and reptiles and set up with Pan to assist you in administering the solution each time the dosage is to be taken. Don't forget to focus on the purpose of the solution as it is being shifted by Pan.

Since you won't need to mask the taste or smell of the brandy, you can just make a solution bottle, if needed.* And, as with mammals, to do the microbial balancing work properly, you will have to do any surrogate follow-up testing that is needed for the Essences Process (p. 29).

* *Place one dropperful (10 drops) of the solution into the spoon for shifting.*

FOR MAMMALS, FISH, FOWL AND REPTILES: When shifting balancers and stabilizers from the spoon in the processes in Step 6, just ask Pan to shift them appropriately to the animal or its microbes (or both)—whatever the focus.* Modify what you normally would say to apply to working with the microbes and/or their host body.

Step 7: The personal solution will be for the mammal, fish, fowl or reptile. Any solution dosage *for mammals* must be administered orally within 24 hours of the program testing if it has not been given directly during the testing for Step 7. (The coning must be opened for this and you must focus on the purpose of the solution as it is being shifted.) Each subsequent dosage is to be given directly and in an open coning.** *For fish, fowl and reptiles*, administer the essences one time during the program testing for this Step with the help of Pan. For any dosages given beyond

** *For all multiple-day essence dosages for mammals, begin the multiple-day count when you begin administering the essences orally. For example, if I am giving a solution to a dog for 3 days, but he's asleep during the testing, I give him one dosage with the help of Pan while the coning is open and the oral dosage within 24 hours. The day he gets the oral dosage is when I begin my 3-day dosage count.*

the program testing, the essences are to be given with an open coning, with the help of Pan—and not directly. Don't forget to focus on the purpose of the solution during the shift. You may wish to make a solution bottle for these essences if a dosage over several days is needed. And you will also have to do the surrogate follow-up testing when needed.

Step 8: Test for a troubleshooting recheck and a date.

Step 9: Close the coning. Don't forget to disconnect from your higher self *and* the higher self of the animal. Then test *yourself* for essences and include a dosage test. This ensures that the work, the amount of focus that was required of you to do the work, the time you spent in the coning and the closing down of the coning have not adversely impacted your balance. (Non-Perelandra essences may be included for this Step.) You do not need to test the animal for further essence balancing. They adjust quite easily to conings.

Be aware of a possible protein drain for yourself and take care of it. The animal will not experience a protein drain.

Surrogate Basic Essence Test for Animals for Step 7

1. I assume you have cleared yourself as the surrogate tester with essences, the appropriate Microbial Balancing Program coning is already open and you have tested yourself again for essences needed because of the coning impact. If not, do so now. (Non-Perelandra essences may be included when testing yourself.) The animal does not need to be tested.

2. You are ready to test for the essences. Place the sets one box at a time in your lap and ask:
"Does _____ (the animal) need any of these essences?" (Test.)
If you get a negative, you don't need to test the bottles from that box because none is needed.

If positive, place each bottle one at a time in your lap and ask if that essence is needed. A positive test response indicates that this particular essence rebalances the animal in light of the microbial balancing work that has been done. Double-check your results by placing all the needed bottles in your lap, and asking again if these are the essences needed.

If negative, retest the other essences to find what was missed. Ask again:
"Are these all the essences needed?" (Test.)

If the response is positive, go on to step 3.*

If negative, you're still missing an essence. Keep retesting the other essences until you get a positive response to the question.

3. For a combination, place the combination bottles in your lap, and ask:

"Is this the combination this animal needs?" (Test.)

If negative, adjust the combination by removing any unnecessary essences. Test each bottle separately, asking:

"Do I remove this bottle from the combination?" (Test.)

Whatever tests positive gets removed. Check the new combination by asking:

"Is this combination now correct?" (Test.)

Continue working with the combination until it tests positive.

4. Administer the essences needed either directly** or from a spoon with Pan's help. FOR MAMMALS: Within 24 hours you will need to give one dose of this solution orally if it can't be directly administered now.

Testing for Dosage

Test for how many days/weeks and how many times a day you need to administer these essences. Animal essence balancing tends to be less complex than what is required for humans, so don't expect lengthy, complex dosages.***

1. Place in your lap the combination of bottles that tested positive.

2. Ask if the animal needs this solution more than one time. If negative, that means the dosage is already completed in the above step 4.

3. If positive, find out how many days you should administer these essences and how many times per day. Do a sequential test. With the needed essences in the your lap, ask:

"Are these essences needed one day?" (Test.)

"2 days?" (Test.)

"3 days?" (Test.)

Do a count until you get a negative response. If the essences are needed for 3 days, it will test positive when you ask, "1 day?", "2 days?", "3 days?" When you ask, "4 days?" it will test negative. That will tell you that the essences are needed for 3 days, not 4 days.

* If only one essence is needed, skip step 3 and go to step 4.

** Place one drop of each needed essence in your hand for the animal to lick, or one drop of each essence on some food. Do not place an essence-bottle dropper directly into the animal's mouth. If you wish to squirt a dropperful of solution directly into the mouth, use a spare, clean plastic dropper. Be sure to wash it well after each use.

*** For all multiple-day essence dosages for mammals, begin the multiple-day count when you begin administering the essences orally. For example, if I am giving a solution to a dog for 3 days, but he's asleep during the testing, I give him one dosage with the help of Pan while the coning is open and the oral dosage within 24 hours. The day he gets the oral dosage is when I begin my 3-day dosage count.

Daily Dosage

Using the same format, ask if the essences should be made available:

"1 time daily?" (Test.)

"2 times daily?" (Test.)

And so on, until you get a negative. Your last positive will tell you how many times per day they are needed. Record the dosage on the chart.

You may wish to fix a solution bottle or a diluted solution in a glass that is to be refrigerated. If you need to make a solution bottle, add *3 drops* of each essence needed to a half-ounce bottle. Then add a teaspoon of brandy or distilled white vinegar if you need to preserve the solution, and fill with spring or untreated water. If this is unavailable, use tap water. Administer one dropperful (about 10 drops) for each dosage, whether it is given orally or shifted by Pan. For a diluted solution, add *one drop* of each essence needed to 2 ounces of water. Then refrigerate. Give the animal 3 teaspoons of a diluted solution for each dosage.

Essences for animals are to be administered in the morning and/or in the evening and/or in the mid-afternoon. If you wish to be more precise, test to see if it is best to administer them in the morning, afternoon or evening, or any combination of the three.

Remember to do the follow-up testing once the dosage for each solution is completed. (See p. 29.)

Gus's Story

Gus is our ten-year-old cat. He's the supervisor of the Perelandra mailroom, and it's fair to say that our staff considers him "whacked out," "a smart ass" and a cat possessed with "a weird sense of humor." I think he's "cheeky" and too cool for words. One day this past summer I noticed a swelling in his right foreleg. I opened an Organizing Process coning for animals and tested that he should have an essence solution for 4 days and be taken to the vet as soon as possible. We learned from the vet that Gus had an abscess. She drained the abscess, inserted a soft, flexible tube for keeping the "drain holes" in the leg open, gave him an antibiotic injection and sent him back home. For the next 7 days, we were to flush the abscessed area with an antiseptic and stuff antibiotic pills down his throat.

It took Gus about a half-hour of struggle to convince us that short of putting him under anesthesia, we were not going to get within ten feet of him with the antiseptic wash and those pills. It wasn't that he was running away and hiding from us. Gus isn't a coward. He stood his ground and threatened to shred us to pieces. We didn't think we'd survive the week, and it seemed like the struggle wasn't helpful to Gus's healing process. I had just developed the Microbial Balancing Program and had been using it personally for several weeks. I decided our best chance of getting Gus through this situation was to forget the antiseptic and antibiotic and put him into the program. He seemed to appreciate the decision.

I opened the coning and began filling out the chart. When I got to Step 2 (identify and describe the issue), it tested that he was to be given a general balancing and that we were to discontinue his first essence solution. That solution had only been for stabilizing him prior to and during the vet visit. (I got this information by asking simple yes/no questions and kinesiology testing.) When I got to Step 5, I found out that we would be working with the viruses and bacteria connected with the abscess and that they were to be tested and treated as a unit. The only process that tested positive for Step 6 was the Essences Process. His solution was extensive—13 essences from all five sets. He was to take the solution 2 times daily for 4 days. He also had a personal solution (Step 7) that was made up of 5 essences and was to be taken for 4 days, one time daily. We made up 2 diluted solutions to be refrigerated, and Clarence took over the chore of making sure Gus got his dosages.

About three days later, I noticed that Gus's leg was swollen again and felt quite warm to the touch. I squeezed it a bit and fluid came out the drain holes. His infection had returned. When I talked to Clarence about the situation, he told me that he had not been able to get Gus to drink the solutions beyond the first day. Gus didn't like brandy. So Clarence asked Pan to shift the solution to Gus instead. I opened the Microbial Balancing Program coning and asked a few questions. I found out that a solution that is to be given orally is different in potency and makeup from a solution that is a nature spirit application. How the essence solutions are applied is not interchangeable. Gus's solutions were to be given orally if they were to be effective.*

I was determined that we could find a way to get the solutions in this cat. Because of the re-infection, I had a feeling that we were now starting over and that the old solutions were null and void, so I started a new chart. This time I wrote "infection and warmth" at Step 2, and we were now

* The NS application that is used for mammals when they are asleep during testing stabilizes the animal for 24 hours, until you administer the oral dosage.

working with his fungi and bacteria. They were also to be tested and treated as a unit. Again only the Essences Process tested positive for Step 6, but this time the solution was even more complex than the first one—16 essences. He was to take it for 4 days, 2 times a day (morning and evening). He had another personal solution consisting of 6 essences that he was to take for 4 days, 2 times a day (morning and evening). I also checked about a vet appointment that we had in a couple of days. I found out Gus needed more time for the microbial balancing to take effect and we were to reschedule the appointment for the following week.

While in the coning, I asked for help with how to get Gus to take the solutions. That's when I got the idea of mixing the diluted solutions in separate bowls and plunking his foot several times in each, one bowl at a time. Being a cat, he'd have to lick his paw clean. I also got the idea of using 2 ounces of chicken broth as a substitute for water to make the diluted solutions and not letting him eat anything else until he got hungry enough to drink the broth. Again, Clarence took over the dosage chores. The paw-lick idea worked, but Gus quickly demonstrated that he preferred the chicken broth approach. So each morning, Clarence gave Gus 3 teaspoons of the one broth essence solution, holding the focus for what it was addressing while the cat drank, and then gave him the second solution in another bowl and held that focus while Gus finished this bowl off.

The third evening into the second solution series, I noticed that Gus had changed dramatically. His eyes were clear and appeared larger. In fact, his whole head seemed larger. He was *present* and, for the first time in weeks, he was playing. I sensed a greater strength and vitality in him unlike anything I had ever seen from him since he joined us in 1988. I knew Gus had turned the corner.

Clarence took him back to the vet the following week. Of course, he said nothing to the vet about how we had tossed aside the antiseptic and antibiotic and embarked on a completely different program. She removed his drain-hole tube, checked Gus thoroughly and gave him a clean bill of health.

When I checked for follow-ups, Gus tested clear. He's back to being his usual whacked-out self and once again takes great pride in whipping the mailroom staff into shape.

Appendices

Appendix A

Kinesiology

Kinesiology is another name for muscle testing. For those of you who use this method for getting information from nature or for testing the essences, you already have the tool in place for working with the Microbial Balancing Program.

For those of you who have never heard of such a thing but would like to use this program, just read on.

KINESIOLOGY: THE TOOL FOR TESTING

Kinesiology is simple. Anybody can do it because it uses your electrical system and your muscles. If you are alive, you have these two things. I know that sounds smart-mouthed of me, but I've learned that sometimes people refuse to believe that anything can be so simple. So they create a mental block—only "sensitive types" can do this, or only women can do this. It's just not true. Kinesiology happens to be one of those simple things in life just waiting around to be learned and used by everyone.

I don't mean to intimidate you, but small children can learn to do kinesiology in about five minutes. It is mainly because it never occurred to them that they couldn't do it. If I tell them they have an electrical system, they don't argue with me about it—they just get on with the business of learning how to do simple testing. Actually, I do mean to intimidate you. Your first big hurdle will be whether or not you believe you have a viable electrical system that is capable of being tested. Here's a good test: Place a hand mirror under your nose. If you see breath marks, you have a strong electrical system. (If you don't see breath marks, call 911—you're in trouble.) Now you can get on with learning how to use kinesiology!

If you've ever been to a chiropractor or wholistic physician experienced in muscle testing, you've experienced kinesiology. The doctor tells you to stick out your arm and resist his pressure. It feels as if he is trying to push your arm down after he has told you not to let him do it. Everything is going fine, and then all of a sudden he presses and your arm falls down like a floppy fish. He is using kinesiology.

Simply stated, the body has within it and surrounding it an electrical network or grid. If a negative energy (that is, any physical object or energy vibration that does not maintain or enhance health and balance) is introduced into a person's overall energy field, his muscles, when having physical pressure applied, are unable to hold their strength. (The ability to hold muscle power is directly linked to the balance of the electrical system.) In other words, if pressure is applied to an individual's extended arm while his field is affected by a negative (energy), the arm will not be able to resist the pressure. It will weaken and fall to his side. If pressure is applied while affected by a positive (energy), the person will easily resist and the arm will hold its position. In the Microbial Balancing Program, the coning answers your yes/no questions by projecting a positive energy (yes) or negative energy (no)—whichever is appropriate—onto your electrical system. The "yes" or "no" you receive in the testing is actually from your coning's projected answer. It is not an answer that has been concocted by you.

When a negative is placed in a person's energy field, his electrical system will immediately respond by short-circuiting or overloading. This makes it difficult, if not impossible, for the muscles to maintain their strength and hold the position when any pressure is added. When a positive is within a person's energy field, the electrical system holds, and the muscles maintain their strength when pressure is applied.

This electrical/muscular relationship is a natural part of the human system. It is not mystical or magical. Kinesiology is the established method for reading that balance at any given moment.

If you have ever experienced muscle testing, you most likely participated in the above-described, two-person operation. You provided the extended arm, and the other person provided the pressure. Although efficient, this can sometimes be cumbersome when you want to test something on your own. Arm pumpers have the habit of disappearing when you need them most. So you will be learning to self-test—no arm pumpers needed.

1. THE CIRCUIT FINGERS. If you are right-handed: Place your left hand palm up. Connect the tip of your left thumb with the tip of the left little finger (not your index finger). If you are left-handed: Place your right hand palm up. Connect the tip of your right thumb with the tip of your right little finger. By connecting your thumb and little finger, you have just closed an electrical circuit in your hand, and it is this circuit you will use for testing.

Before going on, look at the position you have just formed with your hand. If your thumb is touching the tip of your index or first finger, laugh at yourself for not being able to follow directions, and change the position so you touch the tip of the thumb with the tip of the little or fourth finger. Most likely this will not feel at all comfortable to you. If you are feeling a weird sense of awkwardness, you've got the first step of the test position! In time, the hand and fingers will adjust to being put in this position and it will feel fine.

Circuit fingers can touch tip to tip, finger pad to finger pad, or thumb resting on top of the little finger's nail. Women with long nails need not impale themselves.

2. THE TEST FINGERS. To test the circuit (the means by which you will apply pressure), place the thumb and index finger of your other hand inside the circle you have created by connecting your thumb and little finger. The thumb/index finger should be right under the thumb/little finger, touching them. Don't try to make a circle with your test fingers. They are just placed inside the circuit fingers that do form a circle. It will look as if the circuit fingers are resting on the test fingers.

3. POSITIVE RESPONSE. Keeping this position, ask yourself a yes/no question in which you already know the answer to be "yes." ("Is my name _____?") Once you've asked the question, press your circuit fingers together, keeping the tip-to-tip position. Using the same amount of pressure, try to pull apart the circuit fingers with your test fingers. Press the lower thumb against the upper thumb, and the lower index finger against the upper little finger.

The action of your test fingers will look like scissors separating as you apply pressure to your circuit fingers. The motion of the test fingers is

Kinesiology artwork by James Brisson

horizontal. Don't try to pull your test fingers vertically up through your circuit fingers. This action sometimes works but it is not as reliable as the horizontal scissors action.

The circuit position described in step 1 corresponds to the position you take when you stick your arm out for the physician. The testing position in step 2 is in place of the physician or other convenient arm pumper. After you ask the yes/no question and you press your circuit fingers tip-to-tip, that is equal to the doctor saying, "Resist my pressure." Your circuit fingers now correspond to your outstretched, stiffened arm. Trying to pull apart those fingers with your testing fingers is equal to the doctor pressing down on your arm.

If the answer to the question is positive (if your name is what you think it is!), you will not be able to easily pull apart the circuit fingers. The electrical circuit will hold, your muscles will maintain their strength, and your circuit fingers will not separate. You will feel the strength in that circuit. IMPORTANT: Be sure the amount of pressure holding the circuit fingers together is equal to the amount of your testing fingers pressing against them. Also, do not use a pumping action in your test fingers when applying pressure to your circuit fingers. Use an equal, steady and continuous pressure.

Play with this a bit. Ask a few more yes/no questions that have positive answers. Now, I know it is going to seem that if you already know the answer to be "yes," you are probably "throwing" the test. That's reasonable, but for the time being, until you get a feeling for what the positive response feels like, you're going to need to deliberately ask yourself questions with positive answers.

While asking questions, if you are having trouble sensing the strength of the circuit, apply a little more pressure. Or consider that you may be applying too much pressure and pull back some. You don't have to break or strain your fingers for this; just use enough pressure to make them feel alive, connected and alert.

4. NEGATIVE RESPONSE. Once you have a clear sense of the positive response, ask yourself a question that has a negative answer. Again press your circuit fingers together and, using equal pressure, press against the circuit fingers with the test fingers. This time the electrical circuit will break, and the circuit fingers will weaken and separate. Because the electri-

cal circuit is broken, the muscles in the circuit fingers do not have the power to hold the fingers together. In a positive state the electrical circuit holds, and the muscles have the power to keep the two fingers together.

How much your circuit fingers separate depends on your personal style. Some people's fingers separate a lot. Other's barely separate at all. Mine separate about a quarter of an inch. Some people's fingers won't separate at all, but they'll definitely feel the fingers weaken when pressure is applied during a "no" answer. Let your personal style develop naturally.

Also, if you are having a little trouble feeling anything, do your testing with your forearms resting in your lap. This way you won't be using your muscles to hold your arms up while you are trying to test.

Play with negative questions a bit, and then return to positive questions. Get a good feeling for the strength between your circuit fingers when the electricity is in a positive state and the weakness when the electricity is in a negative state. You can even ask yourself (your own system) for a positive response and then, after testing, ask for a negative response. ("Give me a positive response." Test. "Give me a negative response." Test.) You will feel the positive strength and the negative weakness. In the beginning, you may feel only a slight difference between the two. With practice, that difference will become more pronounced. For now, it is just a matter of trusting what you have learned—and practicing.

Don't forget the overall concept behind kinesiology. What enhances our body, mind and soul makes us strong. Together, our body, mind and soul create a wholistic environment that, when balanced, is strong and solid. If something enters that environment and negates or challenges the balance, the environment is weakened. That strength or weakness registers in the electrical system, and it can be discerned through a muscle-testing technique—kinesiology.

KINESIOLOGY TIPS

If you are having trouble feeling the electrical circuit in the circuit fingers, try switching hands—the circuit fingers become the test fingers and vice versa. Most people who are right-handed have this particular electrical circuitry in their left hand. Left-handers generally have the circuitry in their right hand. But sometimes a right-hander has the circuitry in the right hand

and a left-hander has it in the left hand. You may be one of those people. If you are ambidextrous, choose the circuit hand that gives you the clearest responses. Before deciding which to use, give yourself a couple of weeks of testing using one hand as the circuit hand to get a good feel for its responses before trying the other hand.

If you have an injury such as a muscle sprain in either hand or arm, don't try to learn kinesiology until you have healed. Kinesiology is muscle testing, and a muscle injury will interfere with the testing—and the testing will interfere with the healing of the muscle injury.

Also, when first learning kinesiology, do yourself a favor and set aside some quiet time to go through the instructions and play with the testing. Trying to learn this while riding the New York subway during evening rush hour isn't going to give you the break you need. But once you have learned it, you will be able to test all kinds of things while riding the subway.

Sometimes I meet people who are trying to learn kinesiology and aren't having much luck. They've gotten frustrated, decided this isn't for them, and have gone on to try to learn another means of testing. Well, I'll listen to them explain what they did, and before they know it, I've verbally tricked them with a couple of suggestions about their testing, which they try, and they begin feeling kinesiology for the first time—a strong "yes" and a clear "no." The problem wasn't kinesiology. Everyone, as I have said, has an electrical system. The problem was that they wanted to learn it so much that they became overly anxious and tense—they blocked.

So, since you won't have me around to trick you, I suggest that if you suspect you're blocking, go on to something else. Then trick yourself. When you care the least about whether or not you learn kinesiology, start playing with it again. Approach it as if it were a game. Then you'll feel the strength and weakness in the fingers.

Now, suppose the testing has been working fine, and then suddenly you can't get a clear result (what I call a "definite maybe") or get no result at all. Check the following:

1. Sloppy testing. You try to press apart the fingers before applying pressure between the circuit fingers. This happens especially when we've

been testing for awhile and become over-confident or do the testing very quickly. I think it happens to all of us from time to time and serves to remind us to keep our attention on the matter at hand. (Excuse the pun.)

Especially in the beginning, start a kinesiology session by first feeling a few positive and negative responses. Ask yourself some of those obvious questions. Or simply say several times, "Let me feel a positive." (Test.) "Let me feel a negative." (Test.) This will serve as a kind of warm-up and remind you what positive and negative feel like before you start.

2. External distractions. Trying to test in a noisy or active area can cause you to lose concentration. The testing will feel unsure or contradict itself if you double-check the results. Often, simply moving to a quiet, calm spot and concentrating on what you are doing will be just what's needed for successful testing.

3. Focus or concentration. Even in a quiet spot, one's mind may wander and the testing will feel fuzzy, weak or contradictory. It is important to concentrate throughout the process. Check how you are feeling. If you're tired, I suggest you not try to test until you have rested a bit. And if you have to go to the bathroom, do it. That little situation is a sure concentration-destroyer.

4. The question isn't clear. A key to kinesiology is asking a simple yes/no question, not two questions in one, each having a possible yes/no answer. If your testing isn't working, first check your hand positions. Next, review your question, and make sure you are asking only one question. And, while you're asking a question, don't think ahead to the next question! Your fingers won't know which to answer.

5. Match your intent with how you word your question. If you are prone to saying, "Oh, I didn't mean to say that!" when you talk to others, this might be an area you need to work on.

A woman at one of our workshops asked me about some strange answers she had gotten about what to feed her cat. She had asked, "What kinds of food would make my cat happy?" She got weird answers like chocolate, catnip, steak. . . . I pointed out that she probably asked the wrong question. She meant to ask what foods would make her cat *healthy*. She was a little surprised. She thought that this was the question she had originally asked. In short, her question and her intent didn't match.

6. You must want to accept the results of the test. If you enter a kinesiology test not wanting to "hear" the answer, for whatever reason, you can override the test with your emotions and your will. This is true for conventional situations as well. If you really don't want something to work for you, it won't work. That's our personal power dictating the outcome.

Also, if you are trying to do testing during a situation that is especially emotional for you, that deeply stirs your emotions, or if you are trying to ask a question in which you have a strong, personal investment in the answer—such as, "Should I buy this beautiful $250,000 house?"—I suggest that you not test until you are calmer or get some emotional distance from the situation. During such times, you are walking a very fine line between a clear test and a test that your desires are overriding. Kinesiology as a tool is not the issue here. It is the condition or intent of the tester. In fact, some questions just shouldn't be asked, but which questions shouldn't be asked is relative to who is doing the asking. We each need to develop discernment around which questions are appropriate for us to ask.

When I am involved with testing during emotionally stressful times, I stop for a moment, collect my thoughts and make a commitment to concentrate on the testing only. If I *must* test an emotionally charged question or a question about something I have a personal investment in, I stop a moment, commit myself to the test and open myself to receiving the answer and not the answer I might desire.

IMPORTANT: I suggest that you make it a rule not to ask questions like, "Do I have cancer?" Your ability to perceive the answer either through kinesiology or inner hearing is questionable. It is too emotionally charged. If you have a suspicion, get a solid diagnosis from the allopathic medical establishment, and make sure you get two or three "second opinions."

7. If your testing has been going along just fine and you suddenly begin to get contradictory or "mushy" test results, consider that this may not be a good day for you to do this particular work. Or you may need to drink water. If you are dehydrated, your electrical system will feel weak during kinesiology testing. Or you may need to test yourself for essences. The essences balance and repair the electrical system, and this may be just what you need for clear kinesiology results.

What I have included in this material is what is needed for you to do the Microbial Balancing Program. If you wish to pursue kinesiology and develop it for broader use, I suggest that you read the information on the subject that I have included in any one of these following books: *Perelandra Garden Workbook*, *Perelandra Garden Workbook II*, and *MAP: The Co-Creative White Brotherhood Medical Assistance Program*.

Appendix B

Perelandra Essences

As part of the co-creative garden work here at Perelandra, we produce five sets of essences: the Perelandra Rose Essences, Perelandra Garden Essences, Perelandra Rose Essences II, Perelandra Nature Program Essences and the Perelandra Soul Ray Essences. In order to ensure the full range of balancing for the Microbial Balancing Program, you will need to have available the essences from each of these Perelandra sets.

The following is a description of essences and how they are used from the perspective of the Microbial Balancing Program. The steps for doing the Basic Essence Test for Humans is included in Chapter 3. More information on how essences are used in human health and general environmental balancing can be found in *MAP*, *Flower Essences, Perelandra Garden Workbook*, *Perelandra Garden Workbook II*, the Perelandra Catalog and the guides that are included with the Perelandra Essences.

All living organisms have within and surrounding them an electrical network. When an organism experiences "health," this electrical network is balanced and fully connected. When something in its life cycle or environment threatens that balance, the electrical system responds by either short-circuiting or overloading. The organism then goes into high gear in an effort to correct the imbalance. If it does not succeed, it physically manifests the imbalance.

With microbes, essences work directly with the electrical system. By administering the correct essences, we immediately balance the electrical system and stop the domino effect that leads to physically manifested imbalance.

If an imbalance has already been manifested, the essence(s) will then stabilize and balance the electrical system while the organism gets on with the business of fighting off the problem. By assisting this process, essences drastically reduce the time needed for reestablishing balance.

The Perelandra Rose, Garden and Rose II Essences are a natural development in the work that has gone on between nature and myself. They are produced from the flowers, vegetables and herbs grown in the Perelandra garden. These essences are carefully prepared and stabilized pattern-infused water tinctures that are then preserved in brandy. The tinctures go through a final stabilization inside the genesa crystal sitting in the center of the garden. They are bottled in concentrate form in pharmaceutical dropper bottles.

The different essence sets often work in combination with one another. From the human perspective, the Rose Essences address and support the various steps of the process we move through as we face daily challenge and change. The Garden Essences address specific issues on the physical, emotional, mental and spiritual levels that either challenge our balance or arise because of transition. The Rose Essences II address balance within the body's central nervous system, cranials, CSF (cerebrospinal fluid) and sacrum.

The Nature and Soul Ray Essences are made in the Perelandra garden but with a different process. The balancing pattern for each of these essences is not present in any single element or combination of elements on the planet. They are new patterns devically created to address the complexity of today's balancing issues. Although each essence has as its foundation a combination of patterns from existing elements found around the globe, when combined on the devic level (as in this essence production process), the various patterns create a chemical-like explosion that results in a single, entirely new pattern that is not available anywhere else on the planet. New balancing patterns have been created for these two sets of essences without having to create new plant varieties or other natural elements for holding these patterns.

The following are the definitions of the Perelandra Essences. I have not reworded or modified them to apply specifically to microbes and their environment. Rather, they are listed as they apply to humans and human health issues. How they apply to microbes and their environment is related to how the essences address human issues. When working with the Micro-bial Balancing Program, consider that these definitions will serve to simply point you in the *approximate* direction of what is being addressed.

PERELANDRA ROSE ESSENCES (SET I)

The Perelandra Rose Essences are a set of 8 flower essences made from roses in the Perelandra garden. They help to stabilize and balance an individual's expansion or evolutionary mechanisms.

The following are short definitions of the Perelandra Rose Essences.* The name of each essence is the same as the rose from which it is made.

* For full definitions, see the guide that is included with these essences.

GRUSS AN AACHEN: Stability. Balances and stabilizes the body/soul unit on all PEMS levels (physical, emotional, mental, spiritual) as it moves forward in its evolutionary process.

PEACE: Courage. Opens the individual to the inner dynamic of courage that is aligned to universal courage.

ECLIPSE: Acceptance and insight. Enhances the individual's appreciation of his own inner knowing. Supports the mechanism that allows the body to receive the soul's input and insight.

ORANGE RUFFLES: Receptivity. Stabilizes the individual during the expansion of his sensory system.

AMBASSADOR: Pattern. Aids the individual in seeing the relationship of the part to the whole, in perceiving his pattern and purpose.

NYMPHENBURG: Strength. Supports and holds the strength created by the balance of the body/soul fusion and facilitates the individual's ability to regain that balance.

WHITE LIGHTNIN': Synchronized movement. Stabilizes the inner timing of all PEMS levels moving in concert and enhances the body/soul fusion.

ROYAL HIGHNESS: Final stabilization. The mop-up essence that helps to insulate, protect and stabilize the individual and to stabilize the shift during its final stages while vulnerable.

* For full definitions, see the
guide that is included with
these essences.*

This set of 18 essences is made from the flower petals of vegetables, herbs and flowers grown in the Perelandra garden. Their balancing and restorative patterns address issues that we face in today's world.*

BROCCOLI: For the power balance that must be maintained when one perceives himself to be under siege from outside. Stabilizes the body/soul unit so the person won't close down, detach and scatter.

CAULIFLOWER: Stabilizes and balances the child during the birth process.

CELERY: Restores balance of the immune system during times when it is being overworked or stressed, and during long-term viral or bacterial infections.

CHIVES: Reestablishes the power one has when the internal male/female dynamics are balanced and the person is functioning in a state of awareness within this balance.

COMFREY: Repairs higher vibrational soul damage that occurred in the present or a past lifetime.

CORN: Stabilization during universal/spiritual expansion. Assists transition of experience into useful, pertinent understanding and action.

CUCUMBER: Rebalancing during depression. Vital reattachment to life.

DILL: Assists individual in reclaiming power balance one has released to others. Victimization.

NASTURTIUM: Restores vital physical life energy during times of intense mental-level focus.

OKRA: Returns ability to see the positive in one's life and environment.

SALVIA: Restores emotional stability during times of extreme stress.

SNAP PEA: Rebalances child or adult after a nightmare. Assists in ability to translate daily experience into positive, understandable process.

SUMMER SQUASH: Restores courage to the person who experiences fear and resistance when faced with daily routine. Shyness. Phobia.

SWEET BELL PEPPER: Inner peace, clarity and calm when faced with today's stressful times. Stabilizes body/soul balance during times of stress.

TOMATO: Cleansing. Assists the body in shattering and throwing off that which is causing infection or disease.

YELLOW YARROW: Emotional protection during vulnerable times. Its support softens resistance and assists the integration process.

ZINNIA: Reconnects one to the child within. Restores playfulness, laughter, joy and a sense of healthy priorities.

ZUCCHINI: Helps restore physical strength during convalescence.

PERELANDRA ROSE ESSENCES II

This set of 8 Perelandra flower essences are made from roses growing in the Perelandra garden and address the specific functions within the body that are activated and/or impacted during a deep expansion/evolutionary experience.* Although these definitions specifically address the human nervous system, they impact only the electrical systems and whatever systems correspond with our nervous system in microbes and their environment.

For full definitions, see the guide that is included with these essences.

BLAZE IMPROVED CLIMBING ROSE: Softens and relaxes first the central nervous system and then the body as a whole, thus allowing the input from an expansion experience to be appropriately sorted, shifted and integrated within the body.

MAYBELLE STEARNS: Stabilizes and supports the sacrum during an expansion experience.

MR. LINCOLN: Balances and stabilizes the cerebrospinal fluid (CSF) pulse while it alters its rhythm and patterning to accommodate the expansion.

SONIA: Stabilizes and supports the CSF pulse after it has completed its shift to accommodate the expansion.

CHICAGO PEACE: Stabilizes movement of and interaction among the cranial bones, CSF and sacrum during an expansion experience.

BETTY PRIOR: Stabilizes and balances the delicate rhythm of expansion and contraction of the cranial bones during the expansion.

TIFFANY: Stabilizes the cranials as they shift their alignment appropriately to accommodate the input and impulses of expansion.

OREGOLD: Stabilizes and balances the cranials, central nervous system, CSF and sacrum after an expansion process is complete.

PERELANDRA NATURE PROGRAM ESSENCES

The major dynamic of these essences centers around the concept of balance. In balance there is automatic healing. Any living organism cannot be in balance and at the same time be in need of healing. Consequently, these essences focus on shifting to appropriate balance the internal environment of any living organism and its relationship with the larger external environment. With the six V, F and B essences, the focus is on achieving an appropriate internal balance that will automatically adjust a viral, fungal or bacterial imbalance. The Sobopla, Moon and Bowl essences address the balance of a living organism within the larger picture.

All living organisms relate to and interact with viruses, fungi and bacteria both within the organism's internal environment (its body) and within the surrounding, larger environment. Balance implies that their presence has a harmonious effect on the organism. Problems arise when imbalance within the organism occurs, thus causing an imbalance with any specific combination of viruses, fungi or bacteria. As a result, the organism develops health problems that have as their root cause a fungal, viral and/or bacterial imbalance.

The V, F and B essences do not approach an imbalanced, problematic situation from the perspective of eradicating virus, fungus and/or bacteria. They restore internal environmental balance and the balance of the specific viruses, fungi and/or bacteria found within that environment. As a result, you have a vibrant, balanced living organism that includes an appropriate relationship and interaction with existing and surrounding viruses, fungi and bacteria. You will find that when you address health issues from the perspective of balancing all the various elements involved, you will be restoring a living organism to health—be it human, animal, environment or microbe—more quickly than ever perceived possible.

The Essences

V-1, or F-1, or B-1: Restores the body environment to balance when its imbalance is creating a corresponding viral, fungal or bacterial imbalance.

They also restore the body environment to balance once a corresponding viral, fungal or bacterial imbalance is present and impacting the body.

V-2, or F-2, or B-2: Restores a state of appropriate balance within the living viral, fungal or bacterial organisms so that they may once again relate to and interact with their larger host organism (body) in an appropriately balanced and environmentally sound manner.

SOBOPLA (So-bo'-pla): Balances and stabilizes the triangle created by the relationship and interaction between the soul, its physical body and the planet upon which the body resides. As a result, the soul, body and planet become one strong, fully functioning triangular unit. Sobopla also balances and stabilizes the physical seating of the body/soul unit to the planet.

MOON: Balances, stabilizes and, as a result, strengthens the connections and links between specific elements within each living organism on this planet and the corresponding elements that are part of the Moon.

BOWL: Links humans and all other living organisms to the heart and soul impulses of the planet. Also synchronizes the human/living organism with the heart and soul impulses of the planet and the universe, thus supporting the evolutionary process of that organism moving in tandem with the universe into the Aquarian era.

SOUL RAY ESSENCES

Each organism's lifetime or soul ray has a physical body through which its consciousness operates and experiences. The common notion on the Earth level is that a lifetime begins at conception or birth and ends at death. The soul-ray lifetime is much more extensive than this. Its birth/death cycle on Earth is but a small part of the overall range of experience that occurs within a soul-ray lifetime. It may include many different experiences on many dimensions and levels—Earth being just one of its levels.

The soul-ray body is capable of functioning well beyond what is required in a birth/death cycle on Earth. It operates in an overall range that envelopes all activities that make up that full soul-ray experience. What is important to understand for anyone on the Earth level is that this massive array of functioning within a soul ray is occurring in a complex, highly synchronized manner every day.

In order to understand how one organism functions simultaneously on many different levels and dimensions, one must understand that the organism has a far more expansive reality than what we know from the Earth perspective. For example, the electrical system as viewed from the Earth perspective can be defined scientifically as to its properties, characteristics and range of operation. But this is just the electrical system as viewed from the Earth perspective. From a different perspective in the soul ray's experience, the same electrical system includes different properties, characteristics and range of operation.

Perhaps an easier way to understand this is to see the electrical system as a vast, expanded unit capable of functioning on many different levels. Within each separate level, the electrical system operates with only those properties and characteristics needed for functioning within the range appropriate to that level.

The Perelandra Soul Ray Essences have been developed in cooperation with nature and the White Brotherhood to balance and stabilize an organism, from the Earth perspective, as it develops and expands its consciousness. Without this support, the organism's systems can become overloaded and overwhelmed.*

For a better understanding of soul rays and how they function, see the guide that is included with the Soul Ray Essences.

The Essences

#1: Balances and stabilizes the full body as it identifies, processes and integrates its ability to function in a broader, more expanded range.

#2: Balances the sensory system of each level the individual is opening to, stabilizes the system within those levels, and supports the full, expanded system as it functions as a unit.

#3: Balances and stabilizes the interplay and interrelationship between the various pertinent levels of the central nervous system.

#4: Restores the balance and stability of the electrical system on each level that the individual is opening to. Addresses the electrical system on each of those levels as an independently functioning system.

#5: Balances and stabilizes the interplay and interaction between the various pertinent levels of the electrical system.

#6: Supports, balances and stabilizes the interplay and interrelationship between the pertinent levels of the brain. As a result, this facilitates the useful sharing of experiences and information between the appropriate levels of the brain, as well as the corresponding physical body changes that must take place for support.

#7: Balances and stabilizes the refracted-soul heart links and, as a result, solidifies the sense of home base.

#8: Provides the support needed for understanding who one is and one's relationship to the many different levels and activities participated in. Provides the internal support for maintaining that balance.

ESSENCES PURCHASING INFORMATION

Since all five sets of the Perelandra Essences are required for the Microbial Balancing Program, we offer them at a discounted rate in two different sized packages.

NOTE: For prices and ordering information, see the order form in the back.

MBP Essences 1: The Perelandra Rose, Garden and Rose II Essences in the one-dram bottles (34 1/8-ounce bottles), plus the 17 Nature Program and Soul Ray Essences in the half-ounce bottles. (The Nature Program and Soul Ray Essences are not available in dram bottles.) Each set is boxed (MBP 1 includes a total of three boxes) and includes the beginner's guide with full definitions, plus instructions on how to test the essences for yourself and others in your family. You also get a short-definitions card with each box to tape on the inside of the lid for quick reference.

MBP Essences 2: All five sets of Perelandra Essences (51 bottles) in the larger one-half-ounce bottles. Each set is boxed (MBP 2 includes a total of six boxes) and includes the beginner's guide with full definitions, plus instructions on how to test the essences for yourself and others in your family. You also get a short-definitions card with each box to tape on the inside of the lid for quick reference. (NOTE: The half-ounce sets are more economical because the bottles are four times larger than those in the dram set.)

A PURCHASING SUGGESTION: We offer a dram-sized Do-It-Yourself Kit that contains 27 empty dram bottles, labels and a box. If you know someone else who wants to use the Microbial Balancing Program and is also faced with purchasing the five sets of Perelandra Essences, you can share the cost of the purchase. The two of you together can buy the half-ounce size of each set of Perelandra Essences (MBP Essences 2), plus two Dram Do-It-Yourself Kits with 27 bottles each. (The two kits hold all five sets of Perelandra Essences.) Then split the essences in the half-ounce bottles between the two of you. One person gets his essences in the dram-size bottles, the other person keeps the essences in the half-ounce bottles. This way the two of you are almost paying half price for the five sets of Perelandra Essences in the half-ounce size.

NOTE: If you have split the cost of this purchase down the middle, remember that the person getting the dram bottles gets to fill his bottles *twice*. (1/2 ounce = 4 drams. Divided in half means each person gets the equivalent of 2 drams.) So, as he runs out of each essence, the person with the dram set needs to be able to refill each smaller bottle one time. If keeping track of the refills seems time-consuming and unreasonable, you might consider purchasing two extra sets of the 27-bottle Dram Do-It-Yourself Kits (four boxes total) and splitting the half-ounce essence concentrates equally right away. The person with the dram-size bottles will end up with two dram sets of all the Perelandra Essences.

NOTE: If you are sensitive to brandy, you may special order your essences preserved in distilled white vinegar. The prices are the same. Please note your request for vinegar on the order form.

Also, the Perelandra Essences are natural and will not interfere with any medications you may be taking. *IMPORTANT: Essences are not a substitute for needed medical care.*

And finally; we guarantee the integrity and potency of the Perelandra Essences. They have an indefinite shelf life and we preserve them in a brandy or vinegar base to ensure that shelf life. Of course, we can't guarantee mishaps that occur due to "user carelessness," such as replacing a dropper before washing it off after it has touched your mouth or having several bottles open at one time and forgetting which droppers went into which bottles. But we certainly back the integrity of the essences in the areas that we here at Perelandra can control.

Appendix C

Expanded Balancing Process Kit

When the balancers are tested, each one offered is instantaneously fused by Pan with the form's molecular makeup to see which balancer or combination of balancers is needed to improve molecular structure, strength and building. In the case of the Microbial Balancing Program, the balancers that test positive are the ones that provide this improvement.

The Expanded Balancing Process Kit includes the Perelandra Soil Balancing Kit plus the Balancing Kit II containing the additional 18 nutrients, trace minerals and vitamins that are recommended by nature for the Microbial Balancing Program.

The Perelandra Soil Balancing Kit contains 7 organic amendments along with Comfrey Flower Essence. The amendments are: bone meal, cottonseed meal, dolomite lime, greensand, kelp, Nitro-10 (nitrogen) and rock phosphate. These 7 balancers were chosen by nature for the range of what they offer for strengthening and building the molecular structure of not just soil form, but any form. Traditionally, they are used as soil nutrients and are *not for human ingestion*. When you offer them to Pan in the spoon, the needed elements that are in the nutrients are energetically removed by Pan and shifted to the intended area for balancing. This bypasses any need for you to eat a bunch of bone meal.

In the Balancing Kit II, the 18 nutrients, trace minerals and vitamins allow for the wider range of effect and a greater precision in the work that is necessary when working with the Microbial Balancing Program. It includes the following: boron, calcium, chromium, copper, iron, magnesium, manganese, molybdenum, potassium, salt, sulfur, zinc, and vitamins A, C, D, E, niacin and B-complex. (Although niacin is included in B-complex, nature wants the option of choosing niacin within a B-complex combination or alone.)

A NOTE ABOUT THE STABILIZERS: Comfrey was added to the Soil Balancing Kit to serve as an "all-purpose" stabilizer for farmers and gardeners who wish to balance and stabilize soil, but who do not have essences to offer as stabilizers. But for the Microbial Balancing Program, you need the widest range of impact that covers the broadest range of stabilizing needs that are offered by the five sets of Perelandra Essences. They greatly facilitate the stabilization process and enable the person doing the process to understand, through the reading of the essence definitions, what is needed for stabilization to take place. It is in this area of the Balancing and Stabilizing Process that a person can discover patterning for learning purposes.

ORDERING INFORMATION

In order to meet a diversity of customer needs, organizational styles and budgets, Perelandra offers the Expanded Balancing Process Kit as four individually available components.

1. The Perelandra Soil Balancing Kit contains one-ounce vials of bone meal, cottonseed meal, dolomite lime, greensand, kelp, Nitro-10, rock phosphate and a one-half-ounce bottle of Comfrey Essence, packaged in a Perelandra box. This is exactly the same basic kit we have offered for years. NOTE: We list this separately because some of you have already purchased the Perelandra Soil Balancing Kit and shouldn't have to buy it again for the Expanded Balancing Process Kit.

2. Perelandra Balancing Kit II: Hard-to-Find Balancers. Contains chromium, copper, magnesium, manganese, molybdenum, boron and sulfur. Most of these materials are not easily found in grocery stores, health food stores or drug stores. Those balancers in pill form are sent to you in their original unopened bottle, most containing 100 pills.

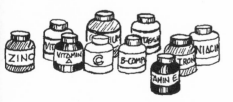

3. Perelandra Balancing Kit II: Easy-to-Find Balancers. Contains vitamins A, B-complex, C, D, E, niacin, calcium, iron, potassium and zinc. If you wish to put together as much of your own kit as possible, you can easily find these balancers in most grocery and drug stores, and you won't have to purchase this part of the Expanded Balancing Process Kit from us.

If you would be just as happy purchasing these from us, we will send them in their original unopened bottles, most containing 100 pills.

4. Perelandra Balancing Kit II: <u>Balancing Kit II Boxes</u>. Includes three 8-slot boxes containing 24 empty vials and 30 labels for the vials. This option allows you to put all of the Perelandra Balancing Kit II balancers into a uniform system for easy testing and convenient storage. (The Perelandra Soil Balancing Kit already includes the same type box for easy testing and storage.)

NOTE: Although the Expanded Balancing Process Kit lists salt as one of the components, we are not providing common table salt. You must supply this balancer on you own. We have our limits!

Here's where the flexibility comes in.

A. If you want to purchase the entire Expanded Balancing Process Kit from us, order 1, 2, 3 and 4 on the order form.

B. If you want to purchase the Easy-to-Find Balancers from your local stores, but don't wish to go on a scavenger hunt in search of the Hard-to-Find Balancers, order 1, 2 and 4 on the order form.

C. If you have already purchased the Perelandra Soil Balancing Kit from us, just order the items from 2, 3 and 4 that you need in order to create the Expanded Balancing Process Kit.

D. If you wish to save money and don't care about putting the balancers listed in 2 and 3 in labeled vials and storing them in 8-slot boxes, *don't* order 4. (The Perelandra Soil Balancing Kit is available only with the box and labeled vials.)

For prices on each ordering option, see the order form in the back of this book. NOTE: We have discovered that prices for vitamins and supplements from distributors change often. We will update our prices on the order form every time we reprint this book, but please understand that we may need to change them in between printings, as well. If there are price changes, we will let you know on the invoice you will receive from us with your order.

Kit artwork by Ann McCaffray

Appendix D

Conings

The central element of the Microbial Balancing Program is the coning. It is set up to ensure perfect balance between the involution dynamic (nature) and the evolution dynamic (the White Brotherhood and you). The evolution dynamic supplies the purpose, direction and definition to any thing or action. The involution dynamic (nature) supplies the matter, means and action for achieving evolution's purpose, direction and definition. The human soul is the force behind the evolution dynamic. Nature is the force behind involution.

Technically speaking, a coning is a balanced vortex of conscious energy. The simplest way to explain a coning is to say that it is a conference call. With a coning, we are working with more than one intelligence simultaneously.

The reason a coning is needed for multilevel processes such as the Microbial Balancing Program is because of the greater stability, clarity and balance it offers. With multilevel processes, we are working with many different facets and levels of intelligences at one time. Consequently, it is far better to work in an organized team comprised of all those involved in the area we are focusing on.

A coning, by nature, has a high degree of protection built into it. Because of the larger scope of the work, it is important to define exactly who and what are involved in that work. All others are excluded by the mere fact that they have not been activated in the coning. In essence, a coning creates not only the team but also the "room" in which the team is meeting. It is important when activating a coning to discern between those team members who are a part of the work to be done and those others who are not involved. The coning is created and activated by us—the human team member. Only those with whom we seek connection will be included.

Members will not "slide" in and out of a coning on their own. This adds to the exceptional degree of protection contained within the coning.

Any combination of team members can be activated for the purpose of simultaneous input. But this does not constitute a coning. A true coning has balance built into it—by this I mean a balance between nature and the human soul. In order for us to experience anything fully, we must perceive it in a balanced state; that is, it must have an equal reflection of the soul or spirit dynamics (evolution) combined with an equal reflection of the form/nature dynamics (involution).

For anything to function well in form, it must have within it a balance between the involution dynamics and the evolution dynamics, or nature and spirit. The extent to which we achieve balance between the involution and evolution dynamics depends on our willingness to allow nature to be a partner with us. To have soul and spirit effectively, efficiently and fully activated into form and action, one must have a balance between involution and evolution (i/e balance).

A coning is set up for the purpose of activating a team for specific work—in this case, the Microbial Balancing Program. It is therefore important for the successful completion of the work that a balance be maintained between the involution dynamics and the evolution dynamics within the coning itself. We do this by setting up a basic coning, which I call the "four-point coning," that lays a balanced foundation between the involution and evolution dynamics.

As a foundation, the four-point Microbial Balancing Program coning maintains the necessary balance between (a) involution or nature, through the connection with the devic and nature spirit levels; and (b) evolution, through the connection with the appropriate members of the White Brotherhood for the Microbial Balancing Program and the higher self of the person working in the coning. We human souls supply the evolutionary dynamic only. We cannot supply the involutionary dynamic.

A coning may be set up for any project or situation in which we would like good, balanced input and assistance. Some people set up conings for assistance in functioning in their occupations. Others set up conings for starting and running their businesses. At Perelandra, we open a business coning prior to all business meetings. With a coning, the meeting runs far more efficiently and decisions are more easily reached. The people who are participating in a coning work with the White Brotherhood to create and hold the appropriate vision and to define and give purpose and direction to all that needs to be addressed. The people then work with nature to come up with solutions and courses of action that best supply the matter, means, action and organization to what they wish to accomplish.

Anyone interested in functioning in harmony with the current transition from the Piscean dynamic to the Aquarian dynamic should include the White Brotherhood in any coning they activate. The White Brotherhood holds the major patterning and rhythms being utilized for this transition. They are part of a balanced coning because they support and assist in ensuring that any work conducted from the coning maintains its forward motion and its connection to the new Aquarian dynamic.

In all conings, we include our higher self to ensure that the work done is compatible with our higher direction and purpose. This input is given automatically by the fact that our higher self is linked to the coning.

The devic connection in the coning ensures that the work being done maintains an overall integrity with nature's design in the area in which we are working. The devic level also creates or designs appropriate courses of action and solutions to specific situations or problems that need addressing. Each coning has in it one or more specific devas. Each living organism and object of form has its own deva.

The nature spirit level of the coning is connected through Pan. We do this because all nature spirits except Pan are regional, and rather than try to figure out which nature spirit or groups of nature spirits are involved in the work we wish to do, we work with Pan—the one nature spirit who is universal in dynamic and is involved in all of the nature spirit activities. Because of this, we do not need to add additional nature spirits to this point. Pan's connection helps us maintain integrity with the laws of nature for all action and issues worked on in the coning and ensures that the nature spirit activity and input is fully represented at all times.

If you wish further information on how to work within conings in your life, I have full coning descriptions and steps for setting them up and dismantling them in the following books: the *Perelandra Garden Workbook*, the *Perelandra Garden Workbook II* and *MAP: The Co-Creative White Brotherhood Medical Assistance Program*.

Appendix E

Perelandra Organizing Process and Chart

Since 1985, Perelandra has introduced a number of health-related processes and programs: the five sets of Perelandra Essences and the book *Flower Essences*, the Calibration Process, the Miasm Process, the Body/Soul Fusion Process, MAP, and now the Microbial Balancing Program. When we become ill or injured, it is often difficult to know where to begin when we take on our own responsibility for treatment. And if Step 4 in the Microbial Balancing Program tests negative—the microbes connected with an issue do not need balancing—you are once again faced with the issue of what to do next. The Perelandra Organizing Process, its coning and its chart eliminate the confusion, guessing, mental pressure and general sense of feeling overwhelmed. They enable you to approach a health issue in a comprehensive and orderly fashion. By opening the coning and testing Step 1 on the Organizing Process chart, you will know which program or process to use first. After testing Step 2, you will know what to do next and in what timing. In short, this process is a proverbial stroke of genius (if I don't mind saying so myself), and you will probably be relieved and happy to include it into your life. (NOTE: I capitalize "step" when it refers to the Steps on the Organizing Process chart.)

As with the Microbial Balancing Program, I recommend that you read this section thoroughly several times to become familiar with the information before doing the Organizing Process.

You do not have to be using all the Perelandra health-related processes in order to do the Organizing Process and work with the chart. If you are doing the Microbial Balancing Program, you are also working with the essences. So that's two of the Perelandra programs you have under your belt. On the chart you will find these options for testing (take a look at the chart at the end of this appendix):

MAP

MAP/Calibration

Microbial Balancing

Essence Solution

Other

If you use MAP and MAP/Calibration, you will be testing all five options. However, if you do not use these two options, you may still test the last three boxes on the chart: Microbial Balancing, Essence Solution and Other.

"Other" is not an insignificant, throwaway box. It connects you with the wide range of health issues, programs and practices that are not covered in the first four options but are included in your personal health regimen. You will need to make a list of these additional options, and when "Other" tests positive, you simply test this list to find out what is needed. Here's a list to use as a start.

Habits: amount of sleep, amount of exercise, type of exercise, water intake, junk-food fetishes, beverage fetishes, caffeine, cigarettes, chocolate/sweets, alcohol, drugs, tv, computer, computer games.

Mainstream physicians: clinic/GP, hospital, specialist, dentist, chiropractor, therapist

Any alternative health modalities that you wish to include (List.)

Perelandra Miasm Process

Perelandra Body/Soul Fusion Process

Perelandra Calibration Process

Herbs (List the herbs you wish to use.)

Multivitamin tablets

Multimineral tablets

Specific vitamins and minerals: A, D, E, C, B_1, B_2, B_6, B_{12}, folic acid, niacin, biotin, pantothenic acid, calcium, phosphorus, iodine, iron, magnesium, copper, zinc, chromium, manganese, boron, molybdenum, potassium selenium, RNA, lecithin, choline, inositol, PABA, bioflavonoid

Diet changes: vegetables, meat, poultry, fish, dairy, eggs, grains, fruits

Home environment processes in *Workbook II*: Energy Cleansing, Battle Energy Release, Soil Balancing and Stabilizing, etc.

Other (Keep "Other" on your "Other" list. If you test positive for this, you are going to have to brainstorm and use your intuition to find out what else is needed for a specific issue.)

USING THE CHART

Issue/Condition: Do not fill this part out until *after* you have opened the Organizing Process coning. Discerning all that gets listed here is part of the process, and filling it out at the correct time will coordinate the focus between you and the coning. Once you have the full information on the issue you wish to address, list it and all the related symptoms that are to be tested with it as a unit on these lines.

Name: I strongly advise you to use this space! The Organizing Process can easily be integrated into a family's health regimen. When you do this, you're going to need to identify everyone's charts, so you might as well become accustomed to using this space right off the bat.

Step #/Dates: The Step number is listed in the upper left-hand corner of the far left boxes. The line next to it is for recording the date you are testing that particular Step.

☐ Integration period needed: If nothing tests positive in the five options across the chart for a specific Step, test if an integration period is needed. If so, check this box. This means that you are not clear as far as the issue is concerned, and, for this next Step, you need time to integrate the work that has already occurred before going on. Start the integration time on the day you are testing and write in this date under the integration box. Using a calendar, kinesiology test to find out what date the integration period is to end and write it in the "thru:" space.*

Sometimes you may open a coning for an issue and the only thing that tests positive is that an integration period is needed. This means that your body needs more time to finish a natural healing cycle it is already in before you add another process to the picture. Wait the full integration time, then test for Step 2 *within 72 hours* after that period has ended.

☐ Clear: When all of your options test negative, this means you are clear

* For each day on the calendar, ask the question, "Does the integration period end on this date?" The date that tests positive is the day the integration period is to end.

as far as this particular issue is concerned. Double-check yourself by testing the "clear" box. If you get a positive, check it and celebrate. If you get a negative, you've missed something and you need to test the options again. If you are stuck in kinesiology neverland and no options are testing positive, yet "clear" is testing negative, you're nervous and/or tense about the testing. Take a break and come back to the testing—within 24 hours.

The option boxes: The option check boxes (the smaller □) are for checking when the option tests positive. When more than one option tests positive, write the number for the order the process is to be done right next to the option check box. (Getting this number is included in the process steps.)

The larger option boxes (in which the smaller check boxes sit) are for recording pertinent notes about what you need to do for that particular process. For example, keeping track of follow-up dates for the Microbial Balancing Program on this chart can be handy so you won't have to refer back to the MBP chart. Keeping the list of essences needed and the dosage information under "Essence Solution" and "MAP" is helpful. And writing down which options test positive in "Other" is also important.

THE SYMPTOMS LIST

To facilitate your testing, you will need to make a symptoms list. The dictionary states that a symptom is "a phenomenon experienced by an individual as a departure from normal function, sensation or appearance." But when considering symptoms, it is important that you not limit yourself to physical "departures." Symptoms also manifest on the emotional, mental and soul-related levels, as well. These are as crucial when considering good health and function as the physical symptoms.

In the traditional, allopathic medical world, symptoms are used for identifying, labeling and categorizing health situations for the purpose of determining a course of action. In the Perelandra programs and processes such as the Organizing Process, symptoms are important tools for determining not only complexity and degree of a problem, but the rhythm and timing of the individual, as well. In other words, we let the symptoms have their full say.

For your symptoms list, write down all your health issues—everything you can think of. This would include recurring problems resulting from old injuries, illnesses or surgery. Add any chronic or serious illnesses or diseases—mental, emotional and physical—that you are currently dealing with or have dealt with in the past. Also add those imbalances that we tend to integrate as "just part of who we are," and then forget about—like bad breath, dandruff, bleeding gums, tooth decay, brittle nails, bunions, unusual moles/warts, eye problems resulting in corrective lenses and allergies (hay fever, poison ivy, bee stings, food, etc.). Finally, add "factor-x," "factor-y" and "factor-z." This will allow the Organizing Process coning to work with one or more symptoms which you have not listed.

The symptoms list will need proper "care and feeding" if it is to remain an effective organizing tool. When new symptoms appear, place them on the list. As old symptoms are eliminated, take those off the list.

PERELANDRA ORGANIZING PROCESS

To do the Organizing Process, you'll need to know how to kinesiology test. As in the Microbial Balancing Program, *all the information in this process comes from its coning* and is discerned by you through the use of kinesiology. Once you photocopy a few zillion copies of the chart (remember to keep one copy clean as a master*), have your "Other" and symptoms lists completed, find a current calendar and get your fingers warmed up—you are ready to do the Perelandra Organizing Process.

You must open a coning to use this process properly. In fact, the coning is the thing that gives the process its "genius." Choose from the following conings the one that applies to you.

a) IF YOU USE MAP: State your intent to open an Organizing Process coning. Then, open your MAP coning using the regular MAP procedure, and add to it the Deva of the Microbial Balancing Program. The statement of intent combined with your MAP coning plus the Deva of the Microbial Balancing Program create the Organizing Process coning.

b) IF YOU DO NOT USE MAP: State your intent to open an Organizing Process coning. Then open a coning with these members: the Deva of Human Healing and the Deva of the Microbial Balancing Program, Pan, the appropriate connection with the White Brotherhood for the Perelandra Organizing Process and your higher self. (Use the same procedure for opening the coning that you use for opening a Microbial Balancing Program coning.)

* The chart may be removed by carefully cutting along the margin with scissors or a razor blade. If you do not wish to remove the chart from this book, you may purchase copies of the chart from us. For ordering information, see the order form in the back of the book.

Use the Organizing Process to test any health-related issue or condition. It will tell you what to do first. Once Step 1 on the chart is completed, testing for Step 2 will tell you what to do next and in what timing. Continue testing Steps until you test clear for this specific issue or condition.

NOTE: If you have been injured, take your ETS first (emergency trauma solution; see *MAP*), and then test for additional essences after the 20-minute trauma period is over. Or, if you don't have an ETS made, test all your essences first. That evening (or as soon as possible) test the injury using the Organizing Process chart to determine if anything other than essence stabilization is needed. If you suddenly become ill and it is not convenient to test the Organizing Process chart, test essences right away. Then test the illness as soon as you can, using the chart to see if anything other than essences is needed.*

* My experience has been to test the Organizing Process chart as soon as I realize I'm feeling "out of sorts." Every time I have approached a situation like this, I have been able to reverse it immediately and completely stop whatever was coming on. Acting fast and dealing with the budding problem in exactly the ways that are needed have been the keys to this quick turnaround.

When more than one option tests positive for one Step (For example, Step 1 might include "Essence Solution" and "Microbial Balancing"):

a) Find out the order the options are to be done. (Do a sequential kinesiology test for the options that tested positive.) After *starting* the first process, *wait 24 hours* and then do the second process. If there is a third process, wait 24 hours after starting the second, and then do the third one—and so on. In the above example, if an essence solution is to be made first, wait 24 hours after *starting* the solution before doing the microbial balancing.

b) Move on to Step 2 on the Organizing Process chart *within 72 hours* after all the options *and any needed follow-ups* in Step 1 are completed. Open the Organizing Process coning and test what is needed for this issue or condition in Step 2. Once Step 2 is completed (including its follow-ups), continue on to Step 3 in the same manner—and so on, until a Step tests clear. All options for that Step test negative and "clear" tests positive.

The Steps for Working on One Issue

** Use the same process to open this coning that you used to open the MBP coning.

1. State your intent to open the Organizing Process coning. Then, using coning option "a" or "b," open the coning. Test essences and take the ones that are needed one time only.** Write the issue you wish to address on the "Issue/Condition" lines on the chart.

2. Refer to your symptoms list, and then ask:

> "Are there any symptoms from my symptoms list that are related to this issue?" (Test.)

If yes, should they be tested simultaneously along with the issue? (Test.) If so, test your symptoms list to find out which ones are related and should be included in the testing. If no, any additional symptoms you may be presently experiencing are not to be included in the testing for this issue and need to be addressed independently at another time.

3. On a separate sheet of paper, make a list of the original issue and any related symptoms. Ask if they are to be tested:

> separately
>
> as one unit
>
> divided into several groups or units (each group to be tested as a whole) Test for which issues are grouped together, which issues might be included in more than one group, and label each group: 1, 2, 3, or A, B, C, etc., for quick identification as you work with and move the different charts through the Organizing Process.

4. Assign Organizing Process charts as follows:*

> Separately: Each symptom has its own chart.
>
> One unit: One chart is all that is needed for the issue and its list of related symptoms.
>
> Several groups: Each group gets its own chart.

* Record the original issue and the appropriate related symptoms for each chart on the "Issue/Condition" lines. Write any assigned group labels (1, 2, 3 or A, B, C) in the upper left-hand corner of the chart for quick identification.

5. Test for Step 1 for all the charts. *Begin testing the multiple charts for the same issue on the same day.* As you test each Organizing Process chart and do the work that tests positive for Step 1, you will note that each chart may be quite different. But they are related, and what each chart has you do sets up the pattern and rhythm of healing between the issue and symptoms and/or the groups of symptoms for this issue.

For each chart, check the options that test positive. If more than one option tests positive on a chart, determine what order those options are to be done in and write that number next to the option check box. When testing for the order of options, treat each chart independently from the others.

If the issue has just one chart (all symptoms are treated as one unit), obviously you won't have to worry about coordination between charts.

6. When *all* the charts that tested for Step 1 have completed that Step, open the Organizing Process coning (*within 72 hours*) and test *all* of the charts again for Step 2. Continue doing this for every Step until each chart tests clear. One chart may clear at one Step, another chart two Steps later and a third chart one Step after the second chart clears. Keep testing the active charts until all have tested clear—including follow-up testing.

If you are working with one chart only, move on to and test Step 2 within 72 hours after all the options in Step 1 are completed. Continue testing this chart until it tests clear—including all the follow-up testing.

7. Once testing for any Step is completed, *close the Organizing Process coning** and turn your attention to the various options that tested positive for you to do on each chart.** IMPORTANT: When working with each option, it is important to remember which issue, symptom or group of symptoms you are working on with this option.

NOTE: The Organizing Process only addresses the organizational part of your treatment. Once you find out what you are to do, you will close the Organizing Process coning and turn to the process, program or medical/health options that tested positive. If they include a Perelandra option and it comes complete with its own coning, you must then open that coning to do that process. *The Organizing Process coning does not take the place of any other coning.*

THE GOOD NEWS: Expect fewer follow-ups when using the Organizing Process. Often, follow-up testing is needed because that is all we are "offering." The Organizing Process coning has a wide range of options on the chart and does not have to address or stabilize a situation with seemingly endless follow-ups—when shifting our attention in the next Step on the chart to another option will do the trick more efficiently.

The Steps for Working on
Several Unrelated Issues Simultaneously

The Setup

Don't do this until you have worked the charts all the way through the process and tested clear for several single issues.*** Tackling multiple burning issues simultaneously without first becoming familiar with the Or-

* If you have used coning option "a," disconnect from the Deva of the Microbial Balancing Program, then close your MAP coning using the regular MAP coning closing procedure. If you have used coning option "b," use the same procedure to close this coning as you use for closing the MBP coning.

** Do not wait more than 24 hours after testing a Step to begin the work that tested positive for that Step.

*** In fact, I recommend that you not read this section until after you have worked on several single issues. Then the information and steps for working on several unrelated issues simultaneously will be easy to understand.

ganizing Process may be an overwhelming and discouraging experience. Familiarity with this process will also help you make a reasonable and well-informed decision about whether or not you have the time and want to put out the effort it takes to address several unrelated issues simultaneously.

1. State your intent to open an Organizing Process coning. Then, using option "a" or "b," open the coning. Test essences,* and list on a separate sheet of paper the burning issues you would like to address simultaneously.

* Take any needed essences one time only. These stabilize you after you have opened a coning.

2. Kinesiology test this list to find out if any are related to one another and if everything on your list of issues should be worked on simultaneously. First ask:

> "Are any of these issues related?" If yes, test the list and check the one that test positive. Then ask:

> "Should any of the related issues be treated as a unit/group?"

If yes, test to determine which issues should be grouped, and combine them on the list. Now ask:

> "Should all these issues/groups of issues on the list be worked on simultaneously?" (Test.)

If no, test to find out which issues should be removed from the current list and worked on later. There may be a pattern of movement through these issues that could be advantageous to your progress if adhered to. List the issues to be worked on later on a separate sheet of paper and save this for future testing. The remaining issues on your list may be worked on simultaneously. This is now your "first list." Use the steps below for working with several unrelated issues to test this list.

3. Close the coning (using the same procedure as outlined for working with a single issue) if you plan to begin the actual work later with the issues on your "first list." If you'd like to move on, keep the coning open and skip step 1 of the following steps.

The Steps

1. State your intent to open the Organizing Process coning. Then, using coning option "a" or "b," open the coning. (Test essences.**)

** Take any needed essences one time only. These stabilize you while you work in an open coning.

2. List the "first list" of unrelated issues to be worked on simultaneously on a clean side or sheet of paper.

3. Check your symptoms list for anything that should be added to the "first list." If something from your symptoms list needs to be added, it means that you didn't realize this symptom was actually a part of these burning issues. In order to address the issues fully, it is important to include this symptom.

4. Find out if any symptoms from the "first list" should be combined with any of the "first list" issues. If so, test each symptom with each issue.

"Should _____ (symptom) be combined with issue _____?" (Test.)

On your "first list," indicate which symptoms are to be combined with specific issues and which are to be treated separately—that is, any symptoms that tested negative to the above question.*

*Be aware that a symptom may be linked to more than one issue. You will need to test each symptom on the "first list" with each of the issues listed on the "first list," and group the symptom with each issue with which it tests positive.

5. Each issue or unit/group gets its own Organizing Process chart. If you are testing two issues plus two groups of symptoms that are to be tested as a unit/group, you will be testing four charts, and you will have to maintain the pattern and rhythm of each chart *independently*—including any needed follow-ups. SUGGESTION: In the upper left-hand corner above the top "Issue/Condition" lines, label each chart A, B, C, or 1, 2, 3, for quick identification.**

** Be sure to include a description of the issue or unit/group on the "Issue/Condition" lines for each chart.

6. Begin testing Step 1 on all the "first-list" charts *on the same day*. Any patterns that may exist between the unrelated issues or groups automatically begin at this point.

For each chart, check the options that test positive. If more than one option tests positive on a chart, determine what order those options are to be done and write that number next to the option check box. Treat each chart independently from the others.

7. Once this testing is completed, close the Organizing Process coning and, *within 24 hours*, turn your attention to the various options that tested positive for you to do on *all* the "first list" charts.

8. As *each* of the charts that tested positive for Step 1 have completed that Step (including all follow-up testing), open the Organizing Process coning (*within 72 hours*) and test that one chart for Step 2. Continue doing this for every Step until the chart tests clear. In other words, after you have started all the "first list" charts on the same day, they are to be tested and moved through the Steps independently from one another until each tests

clear. *Be sure to close the Organizing Process coning once you have completed any chart testing that you need to do.*

NOTE: As when working on one issue only, you may expect fewer follow-ups when using the Organizing Process to work on several unrelated issues simultaneously.

IMPORTANT: Do not start testing a "second list" until *all* of the "first list" charts are clear. Of course, this does not include any unexpected problems that pop up such as illness or injury. These should always be addressed right away.

ADDITIONAL INFORMATION ABOUT THE PROCESS

If you wish to do a preventive general balancing or "maintenance" check, use the Organizing Process chart. You may do this whether or not you are working on other issues at the time. In fact, it is recommended that a general balancing check be done monthly. Simply open the Organizing Process coning, list "general balancing" on the chart and test for Step 1. If you need help, you'll be alerted and you'll know what to do. "General balancing" will be used as your focus for whatever options test positive. If an option tests positive for Step 1, return to the chart within 72 hours after Step 1 is completed to test Step 2. Continue through the testing as usual until a Step tests clear.

When testing for exposure to and possible infection from another person, or if you are surrounded by an epidemic, use *two* Organizing Process charts. One chart is for "exposure to _____ (the dreaded disease) and possible infection." The second chart is for your emotional reaction upon hearing the "joyful" news. You may not have been infected by the disease, but your alarm upon hearing the news could leave you weakened and vulnerable to contracting something later.

If you are presently working an issue through the Organizing Process and you become sick (for whatever reason) or injured, do not hesitate to open an Organizing Process coning and test the chart for that illness or injury. In short, don't think you must wait until you are finished with the process for one issue before taking on something that has unexpectedly descended upon you. If you become ill or you have injured yourself, obviously this is something to be attended to right away. And you don't have to stop the process for any other issues that you may be working with at the time in order to address the new situation.

Suppose you are experiencing five symptoms. Four of them are being tested as a unit for a particular problem. However the fifth one tests that it is not connected with this problem, but should also be addressed now. Treat this symptom independently of that problem and assign a new chart just for it. Then use the steps for working on several unrelated issues simultaneously to work the two charts.

"Other" lists lifestyle changes such as sleep, exercise, diet and vitamin changes that do not have built-in time limits. They are meant to be "permanent" changes until further notice. If "Other" tests for one of the Steps and it involves one of these lifestyle changes, you only need to incorporate the change into your life for *two weeks* before testing the next Step on the Organizing Process chart.

For those of you who have incorporated the flower essence processes from Chapter 8 in the book *Flower Essences*: If the "Essence Solution" box tests positive, don't forget to test to see if you are to include a telegraph test or the two-week process for the issue. Don't assume this box indicates a need for only the basic essence test. (Peeling will automatically test for you when you try to clear out of the basic essence test.)

If you have not worked with the processes in *Flower Essences*, just do the basic essence test as outlined for humans in Chapter 3 of this manual if "Essence Solution" tests positive.*

** Or use the basic essence test
steps as listed in the guide you
received with your essences.
You do not need to open a
coning for doing the "Essence
Solution" testing.*

For the headache of trying to remember all the different testing dates for Steps and follow-ups, I have a suggestion. I put up a small Mylar board. It's located where I will easily see it every day. On it I list the group label or a one-word description of the issue and the date I am to do a test. Then, when I complete that testing, I erase it from the board. Beside each date, I include the day that date falls on. When I glance at the board, I may not know exactly when October 20 falls, but I tend to know the week that includes October 20 and I definitely know when Wednesday will fall.

TIPS FOR USING THE ORGANIZING PROCESS SUCCESSFULLY: You will need to let go of your control and expectations over what you assume a treatment should be. You can't say: "This is my problem. I bet I need a microbial balancing for it." Consider that you don't really know what's going on or what you need. If you really understood this in the first place, you would most likely not have a problem. Let go and let the chart process move you through all the stages, creating the patterns and rhythms that are necessary for *you*. The Organizing Process, its coning and its chart are the tools for carving our path through the unknown, and they give us the confidence we need for moving into and through that unknown.

USING THE ORGANIZING PROCESS FOR ANIMALS

1. To use the Organizing Process for mammals, fish, fowl and reptiles, state your intent to open an Organizing Process coning for animals. Then open the coning listed below. (Wait 10 seconds or verify using kinesiology after each connection is made.)

  1) The Deva of Animal Healing
  2) Pan *and* the nature spirits working with this animal
    State: "I would like to include Pan and the nature spirits working with ____ (animal) in this coning."
  3) The higher self of the animal
    State: "I ask that ____'s higher self be included in the coning."
  4) Your higher self
  5) The Deva of the Microbial Balancing Program

Allow another 10 to 15 seconds for the coning to fully activate and settle in. Test yourself for essences. These will be taken one time only. Also, you don't have to test the animal at this point. Animals automatically and easily adjust to open conings.

The following are the chart options you can test for animals:

Microbial Balancing

Essence Solution

Optional: Nature Healing Coning—If you have a copy of the *Nature Healing Conings for Animals* (printed in *MAP* or as a separate Perelandra Paper*), cross out the word "MAP" on the Organizing Process chart and write "Nature Healing Coning."

"Other": You will have to make another "Other" list for animals that will include all the additional options you are prepared to offer.

2. Describe the problem on the "Issue/Condition" lines. *Follow the steps for working on a single issue as outlined for humans.* For Step 1, test the options on each chart. If more than one option tests positive, find out

See the order form in the back of this manual.

the order they are to be done in and write that number next to the option box. Then close the coning, and *within 24 hours* start doing the options that tested positive as they apply to animals. Once Step 1 is completed for all the charts, open the Organizing Process coning for animals *within 72 hours* and test for Step 2. Do all the follow-up testing for each Step before moving on to the next. Continue this until the animal and the charts test clear.

POINTS TO REMEMBER: I recommend, for your own sanity, that you address one issue at a time with an animal. The timing between starting different options *within* one Step (24 hours) and the timing *between* starting a new Step (72 hours) remains the same for animals. Do all the follow-up testing for each Step before moving on to the next. Continue this until the animal and the charts test clear. Also, you may use the Organizing Process monthly to check animals for general balancing. And finally, remember to close the coning once you have completed any Organizing Process chart testing.

ADMINISTERING ESSENCES TO ANIMALS: Administer any needed essences by giving them directly if you are working with a mammal, or with the help of Pan (by opening a Nature Healing coning for animals* and setting up with Pan for a shift as in the MBP) if you are working with fish, fowl or reptiles.

IMPORTANT: For organizing treatment for plants and different outdoor environments, use the troubleshooting chart in the *Perelandra Garden Workbook II*. How to use this chart is described in Chapter 11.**

AND FINALLY: Do not remove any member from the Organizing Process coning list or add others who are not part of the Organizing Process. This is the coning that has been specifically set up for this process. If you alter the coning, its members will consider the work nullified and will simply wait in a holding pattern until you close the coning down. A non-Organizing Process coning will not function within the Organizing Process.

* The Nature Healing coning for animals includes the Deva of Animal Healing, Pan and the nature spirits working with the animal, the higher self of the animal and your higher self.

** Add the Microbial Balancing Program to the list of options on this chart.

Perelandra Organizing Process Chart

Name: _____

Issue/Condition: _____

Step # Dates	MAP	MAP/Calibration	Microbial Balancing	Essence Solution	Other
1. _____ ☐ Integration period needed Date: _____ thru: _____ ☐ Clear	☐	☐	☐	☐	☐
2. _____ ☐ Integration period needed Date: _____ thru: _____ ☐ Clear	☐	☐	☐	☐	☐
3. _____ ☐ Integration period needed Date: _____ thru: _____ ☐ Clear	☐	☐	☐	☐	☐

ORGANIZING PROCESS CONING:

If you use MAP: Open your MAP coning first. Then add to it the Deva of the Microbial Balancing Program.

If you do not use MAP: Open a coning with these members: the Deva of Healing and the Deva of the Microbial Balancing Program, Pan, the appropriate connection with the W.B. for the Perelandra Organizing Process, and your higher self.

Step # Dates	MAP	MAP/Calibration	Microbial Balancing	Essence Solution	Other
4. _____ ☐ Integration period needed ☐ Clear Date:_____ thru:_____	☐	☐	☐	☐	☐
5. _____ ☐ Integration period needed ☐ Clear Date:_____ thru:_____	☐	☐	☐	☐	☐
6. _____ ☐ Integration period needed ☐ Clear Date:_____ thru:_____	☐	☐	☐	☐	☐
7. _____ ☐ Integration period needed ☐ Clear Date:_____ thru:_____	☐	☐	☐	☐	☐

Appendix F

Focus and Its Relationship to the Human Electrical System

The following session with the Perelandra four-point coning was translated by me on 27 July 1993.

Focus is a natural, organic dynamic of the human life system. It is an electrical function of the brain. Just as the electrical system itself is the physical bridge between the soul and its physical body, focus is the bridge between the electrical system and the physical brain. It can be seen as the bonding dynamic between the brain and the electrical system. Because of this, it contains characteristics of both the electrical system and the brain. And, because of these combined characteristics, focus can have an impact on both the electrical system and the brain. It can function within a brain-oriented dynamic or an electrically-oriented dynamic. In its normal, unconscious state, it functions in both dynamics simultaneously.

The physical brain coordinates the impulses and action of the body. Focus is a physically initiated dynamic that is seated within the electrical circuitry associated with the brain.

Focus can be consciously activated by an individual and used as a tool for accessing, organizing and ordering the impulses of the electrical system. For example, visualization is initiated in the brain through the means of focus. That focus, because of its immediate relationship to the electrical system, causes the electrical system to shift to accommodate the visualization. As a result, the shifted electrical system, which now supports the visu-

alization, moves the reality of that visualization into the central nervous system and throughout the rest of the body. The various elements and systems of the body then alter and modify to accommodate the input from the electrical system. If a visualization has a specific healing intent, the healing dynamic that the intent creates, although triggered by focus, registers throughout the body primarily by means of the electrical system. In short, the body follows the lead/input of the electrical system that is, in turn, consciously modified through the focus that is organized as the result of a specific visualization.

One can see focus as an unconscious or involuntary dynamic between the brain and the electrical system, and one can see it as a conscious probing tool for accessing, modifying and monitoring the state and balance of the electrical system. It is the function of focus to do both. Although a person may not be aware of a focus between the brain and electrical system at any given time, focus is nonetheless operating in order for there to be immediate and quality inflow and outflow of impulses and action between the electrical system and the brain. These two things—the electrical system and the brain—do not operate together in a coordinated manner by default or accident. That immediate and quality coordination is held by focus.

As you can see, focus is not a dynamic that is foreign to an individual and his body. A person does not have to "import" focus from outside himself in order to begin functioning in a consciously focused manner. It is not an extraneous energy or dynamic to an individual. Focus is a dynamic that is as much a part of the human function as breathing. Like breathing, it is automatic or involuntary. Also like breathing, one can consciously work with and develop focus so that it can be modified and function as a tool for the individual to use whenever he so desires.

Many feel that some individuals have no focus, that it is something that has not been incorporated into their lives and experience. This is not true. Everyone has the dynamic of focus fully functioning within his brain and electrical system. It is present and it is functioning, but it is unconscious. To "have no focus" means that an individual has little or no ability to consciously tap into his already-existing focusing dynamic and use it as a practical tool. If a person wishes to develop focus as a practical tool, it would be helpful if he understood that he is broadening the activity of a dynamic that is already present and functioning and not trying first to create the presence of the dynamic, then develop it as a conscious tool. Many have difficulty developing their focus because they spend so much time attempting to create something that is already there. They need only supply conscious intent and simple exercises such as visualization to begin developing focus into a useful tool.

As has already been stated, focus, when used as a conscious tool, can access and modify the electrical system. It is an especially efficient tool for this use because it is already functioning in an intimate and immediate level with the electrical system. A fine focus can access the electrical system instantaneously. A fine focus can access this system in as much a detailed manner as will ever be needed or desired by humans. One need not invent artificial tools for accessing, monitoring and even modifying the system. One need only understand how to appropriately apply conscious focus for these activities.

Each of the flower essence processes that have been developed at Perelandra have been designed to coordinate and activate an individual's focus for specific results when working with the electrical system. Although the flower essences are the balancing and repairing agents of the electrical system, focus is the tool used for accessing the system. Kinesiology is the manual tool for discerning the state of the electrical system. In itself, kinesiology cannot access the system. Only focus can do this. It is focus that opens all doors to the electrical system. And it is through focus that the system can be monitored, modified, balanced and repaired.

Appendix G

About Perelandra and
My Research with Nature

Perelandra is both home for my partner Clarence and me, and a nature research center. It now consists of forty-five acres of open fields and woods in the foothills of the Blue Ridge Mountains in Virginia. The nature research and development has been going on since 1976, when I dedicated myself to learning about nature in new ways from nature itself. I began working with nature intelligences in a coordinated, co-creative and educational effort that has resulted in understanding and demonstrating a new approach to agriculture and ecological balance. Besides publishing materials about the research, we hold annual open houses at Perelandra. *Except for these scheduled days, Perelandra is closed to the public in order for us to have the time and space needed for the continuing research work.* If you wish to visit, write us at Perelandra for information about the open houses.

The primary focus of my work has been the 100-foot-diameter circular garden where I get from nature the information I need to create an all-inclusive garden environment based on the principles of balance. For example, we do not attempt to repel insects. Instead, we focus on creating a balanced environment that calls to it and fully supports a complete and appropriate population of insects. In turn, the insects relate to the garden's plant life in a light and nondestructive manner.

From this work has developed a new method of gardening that I call "co-creative gardening." Briefly, this is a method of gardening in partnership with the nature intelligences that emphasizes balance and teamwork. The balance is a result of concentrating on the laws of nature and form. The teamwork is established between the individual and the intelligent levels inherent in nature. Both of these point out the differences between co-creative agriculture, and traditional organic gardening and agricultural methods. (Information about this work is described in three books: *Behaving As If the God In All Life Mattered*; *Perelandra Garden Workbook: A Complete Guide to Gardening with Nature Intelligences*; and *Perelandra Garden Workbook II: Co-Creative Energy Processes for Gardening, Agriculture and Life.*)

The foundation of the work going on at Perelandra, as I have indicated, comes from nature intelligences, a collective term I use for devas and nature spirits. My work with flower essences and a number of physical health and balancing processes and programs has also been developed from these levels from within a fully balanced four-point coning. The following is a brief description of these two nature levels based on how I experience them.

"Deva" is a Sanskrit word used to describe the intelligent level of consciousness within nature that functions in an architectural mode within all that is form and also serves as the organizer of all that is a part of each form. This means that if I should want to understand or change something in the botanical makeup of a plant species, I would consult with the deva of that species for clarification regarding my specific questions and for advice as to whether my change is viable and ecologically sound. The deva of each type of plant holds the architectural blueprints of that plant and has the power to change the blueprints at any time.

"Nature spirit" refers to the intelligent level of consciousness within nature that works in partnership with the devic level and is responsible for the fusing and maintaining of energy and action to appropriate form. Nature spirits tend to the shifting of an energy reality that has been formulated on the devic level and assist the translation of that reality into form. They also function in a custodial capacity with all that is form on the planet.

As a result of the research with nature at Perelandra, a new science has developed called "co-creative science." Traditional science is man's study of reality and how it works. Co-creative science is the study of reality and how it works by man *and* nature working together in a peer partnership.

Epilogue

by Albert Schatz, Ph.D.

Editor's note:

> *Dr. Albert Schatz discovered the antibiotic Streptomycin when he was a 23-year-old graduate student working for his Ph.D. Streptomycin was the first effective treatment for tuberculosis, the Great White Plague, and for pneumonic plague, the most deadly form of bubonic plague—the Black Death. He initiated the research that resulted in the discovery of the antibiotic Nystatin, which controls yeast and other fungus infections. He has done research on diseases caused by viruses and protozoa; and on cancer, atherosclerosis and multiple sclerosis. Dr. Schatz has been awarded medals and honorary degrees, and is an honorary member of scientific, medical and dental societies in Latin America, Europe and the United States. He wrote the Foreword to the* Perelandra Garden Workbook II *and the Preface to* MAP: The Co-Creative White Brotherhood Medical Assistance Program.

The Microbial Balancing Program is a co-creative health science that was developed by Aquarian research and is implemented in a co-creative partnership with nature. To understand *Aquarian research* requires some knowledge of what *co-creative science*[1] is and what the terms *Piscean* and *Aquarian*[2] mean.

The Piscean Era—which is now ending—has been characterized by a parent-child relationship with nature. In this era nature could satisfy man's basic needs. But nature can no longer do that because of the extent to which (a) we have qualitatively and quantitatively devastated nature, and (b) our population and our needs have increased. In Piscean science we define the direction and purpose of our research and decide how to implement and apply the results of that research without consulting nature in the way we consult one another. In this sense, we work independently of nature. Piscean science cannot resolve the problems that now threaten our existence as a species.

We are presently in a transition period as we shift from the Piscean to the Aquarian Era. This is an era "where man and nature come together," where "there must be conscious partnership," and where "there is need for co-creative partnership with nature in every endeavor of humans on Earth."[3] The Aquarian Era is characterized by conscious team partnership which includes our co-creative partnership with nature. In Aquarian science we consciously establish a co-creative partnership with nature and consult with nature as we consult with one another. We discuss the direction and purpose of our research on which we wish to collaborate with nature, and how we and nature will work together to implement and apply the science and technology which we jointly develop. This collaboration with nature is interdisciplinary research, but of a qualitatively different kind than we do in Piscean science where we collaborate only with one another, but not with nature.

THE REVOLUTION IN SCIENCE

To appreciate the importance of the Microbial Balancing Program requires an understanding of the profound change that science is undergoing. This change is part of the shift of the entire universe from the Piscean to the Aquarian Era. Contemporary science, which is Piscean, includes Newtonian-Cartesian science and the new science derived from quantum mechanics and Einstein's relativity. Co-creative science[1] is Aquarian because it involves a co-creative partnership with nature. This co-creative partnership distinguishes co-creative Aquarian science from contemporary Piscean science. Co-creative science is a unique scientific revolution because it does not fit Thomas S. Kuhn's *Structure of Scientific Revolutions*,[4] all of which have been Piscean. With the exception of co-creative science, all scientific revolutions that have occurred since Kuhn's book was published in 1962 have also been Piscean.

MICROBES THREATEN
OUR SURVIVAL AS A SPECIES

To appreciate the importance of the Microbial Balancing Program, it is also necessary to understand how the global devastation of nature—i.e., *our war against nature*—has influenced the prevalence of some infectious diseases. The imbalance in nature produced by this war now threatens our survival, and microbes are a major component of this threat. The warming of the global atmosphere (due to an increase of carbon dioxide from the burning of oil and coal) has caused an increase in tropical diseases such as yellow fever, dengue fever, and malaria.[5] The global pollution by radiation and pesticides, which are radiomimetic,[6] may be responsible for mutation of microbes[7] that cause some of the "new and reemerging diseases."

Tuberculosis is a prime example of a major microbial threat. "The germ that causes TB is not only one of the most awesome enemies that humanity has ever faced, it is also one of the most unpredictable."[8] Fifteen million people in the United States are infected with TB. One-third of the world's population, 1.7 billion people, are infected with TB. Tuberculosis has killed a billion people in the last two centuries. It kills more people than all other infectious diseases combined. Each year, 8 million people develop active tuberculosis. Each year, 3 million people die. Every minute, TB kills 6.25 people. Because of multiple-drug-resistant strains, tuberculosis may become incurable. The World Health Organization has described tuberculosis as "a disaster of unprecedented magnitude," "a global emergency," and "the world's most neglected health crisis."

AIDS, which is a major problem in and of itself, augments the problem of tuberculosis. Worldwide, more than 10 million people have AIDS. This disease suppresses the body's immune system, which is the main defense against tuberculosis and other infectious diseases. Virtually 100 percent of all AIDS patients carrying the tubercle bacillus develop tuberculosis. HIV-

EPILOGUE   infected TB carriers develop active tuberculosis and become contagious at the rate of 10 percent a year.

CONTRIBUTIONS AND LIMITATIONS OF PISCEAN SCIENCE

To appreciate the importance of the Microbial Balancing Program requires an understanding of the role that Piscean science has played in the global devastation of nature. The following comments concern limitations and problems inherent in Piscean science. They are not an indictment of this science and my fellow scientists. Piscean science has made important contributions. For example, information about the devastation of nature will be used by co-creative scientists concerned with part 1 of the *flipping of the coin.* "In nature" this is "(1) the full discovery of the present state of nature, (2) the full discovery of the healing of nature, and (3) the shift of every molecule from the Piscean to the Aquarian Age."[9] Piscean information that is useful will be incorporated into Aquarian science. Co-creative (Aquarian) science will not replace contemporary (Piscean) science just as quantum physics has not replaced classical physics.

Most scientists are sincere, dedicated, knowledgeable, competent, and deeply concerned about what is happening to this planet, but they cannot implement major changes that are necessary for our survival. One reason is that powerful corporations, with a vested economic interest in the *status quo,* successfully lobby Congress to maintain that *status quo.*[10] But there are other serious problems. Some Piscean science is *iatrogenic science* because, like iatrogenic medicine, it creates more serious problems than those it was intended to resolve. We also have *cigarette science,* which disseminates corporate disinformation for corporate profit.[11] Other kinds of misconduct in science are more widespread and more serious than we assumed.[12] There is also what Irving Langmuir, the 1932 Nobel laureate in chemistry, called *pathological science.*[13] For these and other reasons, one may legitimately ask: To what extent does Piscean science adversely affect the quality of life of the overwhelming majority of people on this planet? And, as a corollary, is Piscean science now responsible, directly and indirectly, for killing more people than the number of lives it saves?

I believe that (a) Aquarian co-creative science offers the only effective antidote to the above-mentioned *diseases* of Piscean science, and (b) many scientists will eventually recognize co-creative science as a qualitatively new and unique approach that should be taken seriously.

PISCEAN ATTEMPTS TO
CONTROL INFECTIOUS DISEASES

The history of Piscean science reveals that it was developed for and has played a major role in business competition (for profit) by exploiting nature. War is an increasingly popular means for conducting this competition. Piscean science developed the weapons of modern war, including the use of microbes as weapons of biological warfare. This Piscean military approach has also contaminated our language. We speak of *The War against Cancer*, *The War against Poverty* and *The War against Drugs*. (We have not yet won any of these wars!) We also speak, in military terms, of infectious diseases and our attempts to control them. "In the West, a major focus of scientific medicine has been the identification of external agents of disease" [mostly microbes] "and the development of weapons against them."[14]

The military metaphor for controlling infectious diseases originated in the 1800s when it was discovered that bacteria *attack* and *invade* the body which then becomes a *battlefield*. This military rhetoric defines pathogenic microbes as *deadly enemies* that *trigger* our immune system. In 1910, Paul Ehrlich pioneered the development of *chemotherapy*, when he controlled syphilis with arsphenamine, an arsenical compound that he called "the magic bullet." The term "antibiotics," which applies to penicillin, streptomycin, and other "miracle drugs," is a misnomer because it means *against life*, all life. Antibiotics are anti-microbial, but not always against all life. Some antibiotics kill certain microbes, but they only limit the growth and reproduction of others. Either way, the diseases then become manageable by the body's immune system.

THE SEPARATION OF MAN FROM NATURE

René Descartes's separation of body and mind (based on an out-of-body experience that he had on November 16, 1619) has retarded our understanding of health and disease for some 300 years.[15] Sir Francis Bacon (1561–1626), the Father of Modern (Piscean) Science, separated man from nature. That separation has been far more insidious than Descartes's separation of body and mind because it resulted in the present global devastation of nature and the threat to our survival. "In describing his new method of investigation, [Bacon] stated that nature had to be 'hounded in her wanderings,' 'bound into service,' and made a 'slave'; and that the aim of science was to 'torture nature's secrets from her.'"[16] Although he deserves credit for having integrated science and technology, Bacon is largely responsible for the scientific revolution to which Carolyn Merchant attributes *The Death of Nature.*[17]

The Piscean attempts to control infectious diseases by waging war against microbes evolved from the separation of man from nature. However, we cannot win that war. Microbes are part of nature and we cannot win the war against nature. Microbes are far more numerous than we are, evolve more rapidly than we do, and readily adapt to the "weapons" we develop against them. We may win battles, but the microbes will win the war unless we approach them differently. *The Microbial Balancing Program offers us a unique opportunity to do precisely that.*

PISCEAN ATTEMPTS TO BALANCE MICROBIAL POPULATIONS

There have been few attempts to control infections by balancing the mixed microbial populations with which our bodies are intimately associated. Commercial preparations of lactobacilli are used to "normalize" the vaginal microbial population that is unbalanced by antibiotics. Yeast infections occur as a result of this imbalance. Some women douche with yoghurt, which contains viable lactobacilli, to control vaginal yeast infections.

Ilya Metchnikoff (1845–1916) recommended the ingestion of *Lactobacillus bulgaricus* to normalize the microbial intestinal flora and thereby prevent production of harmful ptomaines by putrefactive bacteria in the gut. In 1928, G. Papacostas and J. Gaté published a wealth of information on how microorganisms influence one another and how their interactions might be used to control infectious diseases.[18] In 1945, Doris Jones, my friend and fellow graduate student at Rutgers University, initiated a research project that, it was hoped, might identify microorganisms in the throat of chickens that protect them from respiratory infections of viral origin.[19]

CO-CREATIVE SCIENCE
REUNITES MAN AND NATURE

Co-creative science reunites man and nature and thus counteracts Bacon's separation of man from nature. It also provides us with (a) a means of counteracting the global devastation of nature, and (b) the Microbial Balancing Program—an Aquarian approach to the control of infectious diseases. It is fortunate that we have co-creative science as a means of survival at a time when we appear to be on the precipitous edge of extinguishing ourselves as a species. This timing is just right.[20]

Machaelle has been doing important Aquarian research since 1976 at Perelandra, which is a Nature Research Center. Although she lacks the usual academic credentials, nature (with whom she works in a co-creative partnership) considers her eminently qualified. Her laboratory is her garden, where she and nature developed co-creative science. All this was done independently of Piscean science and has not been compromised by it. To say that this is an extraordinarily unique situation in science is an understatement.

CO-CREATIVE SCIENCE IS THE NEXT
MAJOR ADVANCE IN OUR EVOLUTION

Cooperation, which is the co-creative partnership that distinguishes co-creative science, is the antithesis of the above-mentioned competition that characterizes Piscean science. This leads to another important parameter of co-creative science. The anthropologist R. E. Leaky and R. Lewin researched "the common origin of humankind and the basic characteristics—cooperation and sharing—that nurtured our long evolution." They concluded that cooperation enabled our ancient predecessors to survive, and that competition would have been fatal. "Cooperation" they wrote "propelled the human brain toward its unparalleled evolution" and "must therefore be a very basic motivation in human nature."[21]

In other words, our early ancestors survived because they cooperated with one another. Because of the extent to which we have devastated nature, our survival now depends on our cooperating not only with one another but also with nature. Co-creative science offers us an opportunity to work in an interdisciplinary way with intelligences that know far more than we do.

I believe that (a) co-creative science is the most important advance in the history of science,[1] (b) many scientists will eventually recognize that co-creative science is the science of the future, (c) we can ensure our survival only by working in a co-creative partnership with nature, and (d) our entering into this partnership is the next major advance in our evolution.[22]

REFERENCES

1. A. Schatz, Foreword, *Perelandra Garden Workbook II.* Jeffersonton, VA: Perelandra, 1990.

2. M. S. Wright, *Perelandra Garden Workbook,* 2nd ed. Jeffersonton, VA: Perelandra, 1993. Also, M. S. Wright, *Perelandra Garden Workbook II.*

3. M. S. Wright, *Perelandra Garden Workbook II.*

4. T. S. Kuhn, *The Structure of Scientific Revolutions.* Chicago: University of Chicago Press, 1962.

5. "Ignorance is strength," *Rachels' Environment & Health Weekly,* No. 467, November 9, 1995.

6. P. Tompkins and C. Bird, *Secrets of the Soil.* New York: Harper & Row, 1989.

7. J. M. Gould and B. A. Goldman, *Deadly Deceit. Low Level Radiation. High Level Cover-Up.* New York: Four Walls Eight Windows, 1991.

8. F. Ryan, *The Forgotten Plague: How the Battle Against Tuberculosis Was Won and Lost.* Boston: Little, Brown and Company, 1992.

9. "Universal Light Describes Itself," *Universal Light Series 1.* Jeffersonton, VA: Perelandra, 1985.

10. "Ignorance is strength," *Rachels' Environment & Health Weekly,* No. 467, November 9, 1995.

11. "Cigarette science at Johns Hopkins," *Rachels' Environment & Health Weekly,* No. 464, October 19, 1995. Also, M. Zimmerman, *Science, Nonscience and Nonsense.* Baltimore, MD: Johns Hopkins University Press, 1995.

12. *Responsible Science: Ensuring the Integrity of the Research Process,* Volume I. Washington, DC: National Academy Press, 1992. Also, "Washington Perspective. Cool response for Academy's misconduct study," *The Lancet* 339:1219–1220, 1992; "The multimillion dollar academic swindle," *New Scientist,* January 25, 1992, p. 16___; "Perspectives on research misconduct," *The Journal of Higher Education,* Special Issue, May/June 1994; J. P. Swazey, M. S. Anderson, and K. S. Lewis,

"Ethical problems in academic research," *American Scientist* 81:542–553, 1993; and J. C. Bailaar, III, "The real threat to the integrity of science," *Chronicle of Higher Education,* April 21, 1995.

13. T. Patterson, "Cold fusion and hot tomatoes," *Crossroads,* July/August 1994.

14. A. Weil, *Spontaneous Healing: How to Discover and Enhance Your Body's Natural Ability to Maintain and Heal Itself.* New York: Alfred A. Knopf, 1995 (italics added).

15. A. Schatz, "A search for an appropriate philosophy of massage. Part 1: Newtonian-Cartesian Science," *Journal of Spiritual Bodywork* 1(3): 1–9, 1995.

16. J. Achtenberg, "Imagery in healing," *Shamanism and Modern Medicine.* New Science Library. Boston: Shambhala, 1985.

17. C. Merchant, *The Death of Nature.* San Francisco: Harper, 1980.

18. G. Papacostas and J. Gaté, *Les Associations Microbiennes, Leur Application Thérapeutiques.* Paris: Doin, 1928.

19. D. Jones, *The Effect of Microorganisms and Antibiotic Substances on Viruses.* Master's degree dissertation, Rutgers University, 1945.

20. "Timing," *Universal Light Series 4.* Jeffersonton, VA: Perelandra, 1985.

21. R. E. Leaky and R. Lewis, *People of the Lake: Mankind and Its Beginning.* New York: Anchor Press/Doubleday, 1978.

22. A. Schatz, "A network for scientists and engineers," *Perelandra Voices,* 1995.

Perelandra Microbial Balancing Program Chart

Subject: _____ Date: _____

1. Devas of the MBP, Viruses, Fungi, Bacteria, Protozoa, Healing, plus Pan, the WB connection and your h.s. (Test essences.)

2. Identify/describe issue: _____

_____

3. Intent: "I request that the coning focus be directed to all VFBP that impact, are related to or are connected with the above-stated condition or issue."

4. "Do these microbes need balancing?" ☐ yes ☐ no   (If "no," go to Step 9.)

5. Microbes being tested: ☐ Viruses ☐ Fungi ☐ Bacteria ☐ Protozoa ☐ Other   ☐ Tested as a unit ☐ Tested & treated separately

6. Troubleshooting List

_____ Energy Cleansing Process
   Bal: _____
   Stab: _____
_____ Battle Energy Release Process
   Bal: _____
   Stab: _____
_____ Balancing and Stabilizing Process
   _____ Specific microbes
      Bal: _____
      Stab: _____
   _____ Microbes' relationship to body environment
      Bal: _____
      Stab: _____
_____ Atmospheric Balancing Process
   Bal: _____
   Stab: _____
_____ Essences Process   ☐ Oral ☐ Soak with solution (Amount of time needed: _____) ☐ Topical ☐ NS application
   _____ General solution
      Sol: _____
      Dosage: _____
   _____ Solution for specific problem
      Sol: _____
      Dosage: _____
_____ Microbial Triangulation Process   1) ☐ point ☐ link   2) ☐ point ☐ link   3) ☐ point ☐ link
   Bal: _____
   Stab: _____
_____ Calibration Process
   Bal: _____
   Stab: _____
_____ Geopathic Zone Balancing Process
   EC Bal: _____
      Stab: _____
   BER Bal: _____
      Stab: _____
   BS Bal: _____
      Stab: _____
_____ Genetic Balancing Process
   Bal: _____
   Stab: _____
_____ Factor-x   _____ Factor-y   _____ Factor-z   (Bal/Stab each)

7. Personal solution needed as a result of the microbial work
   Sol: _____
   Dosage: _____

8. Troubleshooting recheck date: _____

9. Close coning. Test for essences and dosage: _____

Perelandra Microbial Balancing Program Chart

Subject: _____ Date: _____

1. Devas of the MBP, Viruses, Fungi, Bacteria, Protozoa, Healing, plus Pan, the WB connection and your h.s. (Test essences.)

2. Identify/describe issue: _____
   _____

3. Intent: "I request that the coning focus be directed to all VFBP that impact, are related to or are connected with the above-stated condition or issue."

4. "Do these microbes need balancing?" ☐ yes ☐ no   (If "no," go to Step 9.)

5. Microbes being tested: ☐ Viruses ☐ Fungi ☐ Bacteria ☐ Protozoa ☐ Other   ☐ Tested as a unit ☐ Tested & treated separately

6. Troubleshooting List

_____ Energy Cleansing Process
  Bal: _____
  Stab: _____
_____ Battle Energy Release Process
  Bal: _____
  Stab: _____
_____ Balancing and Stabilizing Process
  _____ Specific microbes
    Bal: _____
    Stab: _____
  _____ Microbes' relationship to body environment
    Bal: _____
    Stab: _____
_____ Atmospheric Balancing Process
  Bal: _____
  Stab: _____
_____ Essences Process   ☐ Oral ☐ Soak with solution (Amount of time needed: _____) ☐ Topical ☐ NS application
  _____ General solution
    Sol: _____
    Dosage: _____
  _____ Solution for specific problem
    Sol: _____
    Dosage: _____
_____ Microbial Triangulation Process   1) ☐ point ☐ link   2) ☐ point ☐ link   3) ☐ point ☐ link
  Bal: _____
  Stab: _____
_____ Calibration Process
  Bal: _____
  Stab: _____
_____ Geopathic Zone Balancing Process
  EC Bal: _____
    Stab: _____
  BER Bal: _____
    Stab: _____
  BS Bal: _____
    Stab: _____
_____ Genetic Balancing Process
  Bal: _____
  Stab: _____
_____ Factor-x   _____ Factor-y   _____ Factor-z (Bal/Stab each)

7. Personal solution needed as a result of the microbial work
  Sol: _____
  Dosage: _____

8. Troubleshooting recheck date: _____

9. Close coning. Test for essences and dosage: _____

Perelandra Microbial Balancing Program Chart

Subject: _____ Date: _____

1. Devas of the MBP, Viruses, Fungi, Bacteria, Protozoa, Healing, plus Pan, the WB connection and your h.s. (Test essences.)

2. Identify/describe issue: _____
   _____

3. Intent: "I request that the coning focus be directed to all VFBP that impact, are related to or are connected with the above-stated condition or issue."

4. "Do these microbes need balancing?" ☐ yes ☐ no   (If "no," go to Step 9.)

5. Microbes being tested: ☐ Viruses ☐ Fungi ☐ Bacteria ☐ Protozoa ☐ Other   ☐ Tested as a unit ☐ Tested & treated separately

6. Troubleshooting List

____ Energy Cleansing Process
    Bal: _____
    Stab: _____

____ Battle Energy Release Process
    Bal: _____
    Stab: _____

____ Balancing and Stabilizing Process
    ____ Specific microbes
        Bal: _____
        Stab: _____
    ____ Microbes' relationship to body environment
        Bal: _____
        Stab: _____

____ Atmospheric Balancing Process
    Bal: _____
    Stab: _____

____ Essences Process   ☐ Oral ☐ Soak with solution (Amount of time needed: _____) ☐ Topical ☐ NS application
    ____ General solution
        Sol: _____
        Dosage: _____
    ____ Solution for specific problem
        Sol: _____
        Dosage: _____

____ Microbial Triangulation Process   1) ☐ point ☐ link   2) ☐ point ☐ link   3) ☐ point ☐ link
    Bal: _____
    Stab: _____

____ Calibration Process
    Bal: _____
    Stab: _____

____ Geopathic Zone Balancing Process
    EC Bal: _____
        Stab: _____
    BER Bal: _____
        Stab: _____
    BS Bal: _____
        Stab: _____

____ Genetic Balancing Process
    Bal: _____
    Stab: _____
____ Factor-x   ____ Factor-y   ____ Factor-z   (Bal/Stab each)

7. Personal solution needed as a result of the microbial work
    Sol: _____
    Dosage: _____

8. Troubleshooting recheck date: _____

9. Close coning. Test for essences and dosage: _____

Perelandra Microbial Balancing Program Chart

Subject: _____ Date: _____

1. Devas of the MBP, Viruses, Fungi, Bacteria, Protozoa, Healing, plus Pan, the WB connection and your h.s. (Test essences.)

2. Identify/describe issue: _____
   _____

3. Intent: "I request that the coning focus be directed to all VFBP that impact, are related to or are connected with the above-stated condition or issue."

4. "Do these microbes need balancing?" ☐ yes ☐ no   (If "no," go to Step 9.)

5. Microbes being tested: ☐ Viruses ☐ Fungi ☐ Bacteria ☐ Protozoa ☐ Other   ☐ Tested as a unit ☐ Tested & treated separately

6. Troubleshooting List

____ Energy Cleansing Process
   Bal: _____
   Stab: _____

____ Battle Energy Release Process
   Bal: _____
   Stab: _____

____ Balancing and Stabilizing Process
   ____ Specific microbes
      Bal: _____
      Stab: _____
   ____ Microbes' relationship to body environment
      Bal: _____
      Stab: _____

____ Atmospheric Balancing Process
   Bal: _____
   Stab: _____

____ Essences Process   ☐ Oral ☐ Soak with solution (Amount of time needed: _____) ☐ Topical ☐ NS application
   ____ General solution
      Sol: _____
      Dosage: _____
   ____ Solution for specific problem
      Sol: _____
      Dosage: _____

____ Microbial Triangulation Process   1) ☐ point ☐ link   2) ☐ point ☐ link   3) ☐ point ☐ link
   Bal: _____
   Stab: _____

____ Calibration Process
   Bal: _____
   Stab: _____

____ Geopathic Zone Balancing Process
   EC Bal: _____
      Stab: _____
   BER Bal: _____
      Stab: _____
   BS Bal: _____
      Stab: _____

____ Genetic Balancing Process
   Bal: _____
   Stab: _____

____ Factor-x   ____ Factor-y   ____ Factor-z   (Bal/Stab each)

7. Personal solution needed as a result of the microbial work
   Sol: _____
   Dosage: _____

8. Troubleshooting recheck date: _____

9. Close coning. Test for essences and dosage: _____

Perelandra Microbial Balancing Program Chart

Subject: _____ Date: _____

1. Devas of the MBP, Viruses, Fungi, Bacteria, Protozoa, Healing, plus Pan, the WB connection and your h.s. (Test essences.)

2. Identify/describe issue: _____
   _____

3. Intent: "I request that the coning focus be directed to all VFBP that impact, are related to or are connected with the above-stated condition or issue."

4. "Do these microbes need balancing?" ☐ yes ☐ no   (If "no," go to Step 9.)

5. Microbes being tested: ☐ Viruses ☐ Fungi ☐ Bacteria ☐ Protozoa ☐ Other   ☐ Tested as a unit ☐ Tested & treated separately

6. Troubleshooting List

_____ Energy Cleansing Process
     Bal: _____
     Stab: _____
_____ Battle Energy Release Process
     Bal: _____
     Stab: _____
_____ Balancing and Stabilizing Process
     _____ Specific microbes
         Bal: _____
         Stab: _____
     _____ Microbes' relationship to body environment
         Bal: _____
         Stab: _____
_____ Atmospheric Balancing Process
     Bal: _____
     Stab: _____
_____ Essences Process   ☐ Oral ☐ Soak with solution (Amount of time needed: _____) ☐ Topical ☐ NS application
     _____ General solution
         Sol: _____
         Dosage: _____
     _____ Solution for specific problem
         Sol: _____
         Dosage: _____
_____ Microbial Triangulation Process   1) ☐ point ☐ link   2) ☐ point ☐ link   3) ☐ point ☐ link
     Bal: _____
     Stab: _____
_____ Calibration Process
     Bal: _____
     Stab: _____
_____ Geopathic Zone Balancing Process
     EC Bal: _____
        Stab: _____
     BER Bal: _____
        Stab: _____
     BS Bal: _____
        Stab: _____
_____ Genetic Balancing Process
     Bal: _____
     Stab: _____
_____ Factor-x   _____ Factor-y   _____ Factor-z   (Bal/Stab each)

7. Personal solution needed as a result of the microbial work
     Sol: _____
     Dosage: _____

8. Troubleshooting recheck date: _____

9. Close coning. Test for essences and dosage: _____

PERELANDRA
P.O. Box 3603
Warrenton, VA 20188
24-Hour Phone: (540) 937-2153
24-Hour Fax Number: (540) 937-3360

MBP Order Form

A complete listing of all Perelandra products is included in our free catalog,
which is sent upon request. Prices in this order form are subject to change.

___ *Perelandra Garden Workbook* B-103 . . . . $19.95

___ *Perelandra Garden Workbook II* B-105 . . . . $16.95

___ *Perelandra Garden Workbook* and *Workbook II* (together @ 20% discount) B-135 . . . . $29.52

___ *MAP* B-106 . . . . $14.95

___ *Flower Essences* B-104 . . . . $10.95

___ *Dancing in the Shadows of the Moon* (hard cover) B-107 . . . . $23

___ *Behaving As If the God in All Life Mattered* B-101 . . . . $9.95

___ *Microbial Balancing Program Manual* B-108 . . . . $16

Expanded Balancing Process Kit options: (See p. 130 for ordering information.)

      ___ 1. Perelandra Soil Balancing Kit G-101 . . . . $14.95

      ___ Perelandra Balancing Kit II (Includes 2, 3, and 4 at a $20 discount) G-401 . . . . $120

      ___ 2. Hard-to-Find Balancers G-402 . . . . $40

      ___ 3. Easy-to-Find Balancers G-403 . . . . $80

      ___ 4. Balancing Kit II Boxes G-404 . . . . $20

The five sets of Perelandra Essences: (See p. 127 for ordering information.)

      ___ MBP Essences I: Rose I, Garden and Rose II Essences in dram bottles, Nature
            Program and Soul Ray in half-ounce bottles E-601 . . . . $165

      ___ MBP Essences II: all five sets in half-ounce bottles E-602 . . . . $205

      ___ *Please preserve my essences in vinegar instead of brandy.*

___ Do-It-Yourself Kit: 27 dram bottles (2 Kits fit all five essence sets) E-402 . . . . $24 ea.

___ Solution bottles: 1/2-ounce only E-401 . . . . 85¢ each

      *NOTE: If you wish to purchase the Perelandra Essences as separate sets
      or as individual bottles, please see our catalog for listings and prices.*

___ Microbial Balancing Program Charts (50 charts) G-203 . . . . $5

___ Organizing Process Charts (50 charts) G-204 . . . . $5

Perelandra Papers . . . . $2 each

      ___ # 2—*Calibration Process* (This paper is included in *MAP*.) P-202

      ___ # 3—*Miasms* P-203

      ___ # 4—*Body/Soul Fusion Process* P-204

      ___ # 8—*Nature Healing Conings for Animals* (This paper is included in *MAP*.) P-208

Please print more clearly than you ever have in your entire life.

QTY	STOCK #	DESCRIPTION	UNIT PRICE		TOTAL PRICE	

☐ *Please preserve my essences in vinegar instead of brandy.*

☐ *Send additional catalog(s). Qty: ____*

Subtotal				
− 15% Senior Discount				
+ VA Tax: 4-1/2%*				
+ Shipping & Handling				
TOTAL				

* VA residents only.

U.S. Postage & Handling (See our catalog for international rates.)

Thru $7 . . . . $2.10
$7.01 to 10.00 . . . . . $3.15
$10.01 to 14.00 . . . . $4.20
$14.01 to 25.00 . . . . $4.80
$25.01 to 50.00 . . . . $5.80
$50.01 to 75.00 . . . . $7.00
$75.01 to 100.00 . . . $8.00
$100.01 to 200.00 . . $9.00
$200.01 to 300.00 . . $11.00
$300.01 and over. . . 5% of order

- AK and HI: If total is over $10, please send 1-1/2 times chart. (Will be shipped 1st class.)

- UPS—2nd Day Air: add $6 to postage, except AK and HI: add $9.

- UPS—Next Day Air: add $20 to postage, except AK and HI: add $25. (Next Day orders over $200 may be more. If so, we will bill.)

- NOTE: Prices and shipping charges subject to change without notice.

METHOD OF PAYMENT

☐ Check ☐ Money Order ☐ Visa ☐ MasterCard ☐ Discover ☐ Gift Certificate

Name: _____

UPS Address: _____

_____

City/State & Zip: _____

Daytime phone: _____

Credit Card Number: _____

Expiration Date: _____ / _____ / _____

Signature: _____